I'm convinced that the Bible is somehow powerfully simpl[e] [and] complex. Like a diamond viewed from different angles, Scripture continually confronts my heart in fresh ways. This Bible-study series offers insightful perspectives and gives its participants a refreshing opportunity to admire the character of God and be transformed by the truth of his Word. Our souls need to meander through the minutiae and metanarrative of the Bible, and the **Storyline Bible Studies** help us do both.

> KYLE IDLEMAN, senior pastor of Southeast Christian Church and bestselling author of *Not a Fan* and *One at a Time*

If you are longing for a breath of fresh air in your spiritual life, this study is for you. Kat Armstrong brings to life both familiar and less familiar Bible stories in such an engaging way that you can't help but see how the God of the past is also working and moving in your present. Through the captivating truths revealed in this series, you will discover more about God's faithfulness, be equipped to move past fear and disappointment, and be empowered to be who you were created to be. If your faith has felt mundane or routine, these words will be a refreshing balm to your soul and a guide to go deeper in your relationship with God.

> HOSANNA WONG, international speaker and bestselling author of *How (Not) to Save the World: The Truth about Revealing God's Love to the People Right Next to You*

We are watching a new wave of Bible studies that care about the Bible's big story, from Genesis to Revelation; that plunge Bible readers into the depths of human despair and show them the glories of the Kingdom God plans for creation; and that invite readers to participate in that story in all its dimensions—in the mountains and the valleys. Anyone who ponders these Bible studies will come to terms not only with the storyline of the Bible but also with where each of us fits in God's grand narrative. I heartily commend Kat's **Storyline Bible Studies**.

> REV. CANON DR. SCOT MCKNIGHT, professor of New Testament at Northern Seminary

Kat Armstrong is an able trail guide with contagious enthusiasm! In this series, she'll take you hiking through Scripture to experience mountains and valleys, sticks and stones, sinners and saints. If you are relatively new to the Bible or are struggling to see how it all fits together, your trek with Kat will be well worth it. You might even decide that hiking through the Bible is your new hobby.

CARMEN JOY IMES, associate professor of Old Testament at Biola University and author of *Bearing God's Name: Why Sinai Still Matters*

Kat Armstrong takes you into the heart of Scripture so that Scripture can grow in your heart. The **Storyline Bible Studies** have everything: the overarching story of God's redemption, the individual biblical story's historical context, and the text's interpretation that connects with today's realities. Armstrong asks insightful questions that make the Bible come alive and draws authentically on her own faith journey so that readers might deepen their relationship with Jesus. Beautifully written and accessible, the **Storyline Bible Studies** are a wonderful resource for individual or group study.

LYNN H. COHICK, PHD, provost and dean of academic affairs at Northern Seminary

Christians affirm that the Bible is God's Word and provides God's life-giving instruction and encouragement. But what good is such an authoritative and valuable text if God's people don't engage it to find the help the Scriptures provide? Here's where Kat Armstrong's studies shine. In each volume, she presents Bible study as a journey through Scripture that can be transformational. In the process, she enables readers to see the overarching storyline of the Bible and to find their place in that story. In addition, Armstrong reinforces the essential steps that make Bible study life-giving for people seeking to grow in their faith. Whether for individuals, for small groups, or as part of a church curriculum, these studies are ideally suited to draw students into a fresh and invigorating engagement with God's Word.

WILLIAM W. KLEIN, PHD, professor emeritus of New Testament interpretation and author of *Handbook for Personal Bible Study: Enriching Your Experience with God's Word*

Kat has done two things that I love. She's taken something that is familiar and presented it in a fresh way that is understandable by all, balancing the profound with accessibility. And her trustworthy and constant approach to Bible study equips the participant to emerge from this study with the ability to keep studying and growing more.

MARTY SOLOMON, creator and executive producer of *The BEMA Podcast*

You are in for an adventure. In this series, Kat pulls back the curtain to reveal how intentionally God has woven together seemingly disconnected moments in the collective Bible story. Her delivery is both brilliant and approachable. She will invite you to be a curious sleuth as you navigate familiar passages of Scripture, discovering things you'd never seen before. I promise you will never read the living Word the same again.

JENN JETT BARRETT, founder and visionary of The Well Summit

Kat has done it again! The same wisdom, depth, humility, and authenticity that we have come to expect from her previous work is on full display here in her new **Storyline Bible Study** series. Kat is the perfect guide through these important themes and through the story of Scripture: gentle and generous on the one hand, capable and clear on the other. She is a gifted communicator and teacher of God's Word. The format of these studies is helpful too— perfect pacing, just the right amount of new information at each turn, with plenty of space for writing and prayerful reflection as you go and some great resources for further study. I love learning from Kat, and I'm sure you will too. Grab a few friends from your church or neighborhood and dig into these incredible resources together to find your imagination awakened and your faith strengthened.

DAN LOWERY, president of Pillar Seminary

Kat Armstrong possesses something I deeply admire: a sincere and abiding respect for the Bible. Her tenaciousness to know more about her beloved Christ, her commitment to truth telling, and her desire to dig until she mines the deepest gold for her Bible-study readers makes her one of my favorite Bible teachers. I find few that match her scriptural attentiveness and even fewer that embody her humble spirit. This project is stunning, like the rest of her work.

LISA WHITTLE, bestselling author of *Jesus over Everything: Uncomplicating the Daily Struggle to Put Jesus First*, Bible teacher, and podcast host

STICKS

ROOTING YOUR FAITH IN GODLY WISDOM
WHEN YOUR DECISIONS MATTER THE MOST

KAT ARMSTRONG

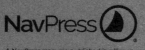

A NavPress resource published in alliance
with Tyndale House Publishers

NavPress ◖

NavPress is the publishing ministry of The Navigators, an international Christian organization and leader in personal spiritual development. NavPress is committed to helping people grow spiritually and enjoy lives of meaning and hope through personal and group resources that are biblically rooted, culturally relevant, and highly practical.

For more information, visit NavPress.com.

Sticks: Rooting Your Faith in Godly Wisdom When Your Decisions Matter the Most

Copyright © 2023 by Kat Armstrong. All rights reserved.

A NavPress resource published in alliance with Tyndale House Publishers

NavPress and the NavPress logo are registered trademarks of NavPress, The Navigators, Colorado Springs, CO. *Tyndale* is a registered trademark of Tyndale House Ministries. Absence of ® in connection with marks of NavPress or other parties does not indicate an absence of registration of those marks.

The Team:
David Zimmerman, Publisher; Caitlyn Carlson, Acquisitions Editor; Elizabeth Schroll, Copy Editor; Olivia Eldredge, Operations Manager; Julie Chen, Designer; Sarah K. Johnson, Proofreader

Cover illustration by Lindsey Bergsma. Copyright © 2023 by NavPress/The Navigators. All rights reserved.

Author photo by Jody Rodriguez, copyright © 2021. All rights reserved.

Author is represented by Jana Burson of The Christopher Ferebee Agency, christopherferebee.com

For information about special discounts for bulk purchases, please contact Tyndale House Publishers at csresponse@tyndale.com, or call 1-855-277-9400.

ISBN 978-1-64158-588-0

Printed in the United States of America

29	28	27	26	25	24	23
7	6	5	4	3	2	1

For my dad, Ronald K. Obenhaus.
I think you would have loved this.

Contents

A Message from Kat

THE BIBLE IS a literary masterpiece.

Whether you are new to the Christian faith or a seasoned Bible reader, I wrote the **Storyline Bible Studies** to guide you through the storyline of Scripture—each following a person, place, or thing in the Bible. Maybe you are practiced in dissecting a passage or verse and pulling things out of the text to apply to your life. But now you may feel as though your faith is fragmented, coming apart at the seams. The **Storyline Bible Studies** will help you put things back together. You'll discover cohesive, thematic storylines with literary elements and appreciate the Bible as the literary masterpiece that it is.

Tracing a biblical theme, with imagery like mountains and valleys or sticks and stones, will spark your holy curiosity and empower you to cultivate a biblical imagination. I'm praying that your time studying God's Word is an awe-inspiring catalyst to engage and experience God's truth—that you will marvel at the artistry of God's storytelling. And that the Bible will never feel dull or boring ever again.

I wrote *Sticks* when my whole life felt like one big decision tree. If there was an existential question about my career, my family, or our future, we were asking it. We made more big decisions then than in any other season of our twenty-year marriage. And each time I made a hard choice, the stakes felt high and my faith was tested.

I needed God's wisdom—his help in discerning what to do regarding the weighty decisions. And when the next right step seemed clear, I needed the Spirit's empowerment to follow through. So I began to look for stories in the Bible where people were seeking God's wisdom, making hard choices, or finding their faith tested, knowing that God would illuminate my own story through studying.

As I spent time meditating on Adam and Eve's story in the Garden of Eden, I noticed the beginning of a pattern in Scripture. Adam and Eve's big decision happened near two trees: the Tree of Life and the Tree of the Knowledge of Good and Evil. And as I explored further, searching for guidance in stories where people had to make choices with lasting impact . . . I found more trees.

If you're struggling with decision fatigue, studying the trees in the Bible will help you prioritize the decisions that need your attention. All the little choices will take up less brain space because you'll be able to focus on what really matters.

If you're looking for wisdom, studying trees in the Bible will root you deeply in the Source of wisdom. Many of the people in our faith history faced hard choices, too, and their successes and failures can be our teacher.

I'm praying your time studying trees in the Bible is an awe-inspiring catalyst to engage and experience God's truth—that you would marvel at the artistry of God's storytelling. And that the trees in the Bible will connect you to the Tree of Life, enabling you to live wisely and to make hard choices that honor God.

Love,

Kat

The Storyline of Scripture

YOUR DECISION TO STUDY THE BIBLE for the next few weeks is no accident—God has brought you here, to this moment. And I don't want to take it for granted. Here, at the beginning, I want to invite you into the most important step you can take, the one that brings the whole of the Bible alive in extraordinary ways: a relationship with Jesus.

The Bible is a collection of divinely inspired manuscripts written over fifteen hundred years by at least forty different authors. Together, the manuscripts make up tens of thousands of verses, sixty-six books, and two testaments. Point being: It's a lot of content.

But the Bible is really just one big story: God's story of redemption. From Genesis to Revelation the Bible includes narratives, songs, poems, wisdom literature, letters, and even apocalyptic prophecies. Yet everything we read in God's Word helps us understand God's love and his plan to be in a relationship with us.

If you hear nothing else, hear this: God loves you.

It's easy to get lost in the vast amount of information in the Bible, so we're going to explore the storyline of Scripture in four parts. And as you locate your experience in the story of the Bible, I hope the story of redemption becomes your own.

PART 1: GOD MADE SOMETHING GOOD.

The big story—God's story of redemption—started in a garden. When God launched his project for humanity, he purposed all of us—his image bearers—to flourish and co-create with him. In the beginning there was peace, beauty, order, and abundant life. The soil was good. Life was good. We rarely hear this part of our story, but it doesn't make it less true. God created something good—and that includes you.

PART 2: WE MESSED IT UP.

If you've ever thought, *This isn't how it's supposed to be*, you're right. It's not. We messed up God's good world. Do you ever feel like you've won gold medals in messing things up? Me too. All humanity shares in that brokenness. We are imperfect. The people we love are imperfect. Our systems are jacked, and our world is broken. And that's on us. We made the mess, and we literally can't help ourselves. We need to be rescued from our circumstances, the systems in which we live, and ourselves.

PART 3: JESUS MAKES IT RIGHT.

The good news is that God can clean up all our messes, and he does so through the life, death, and resurrection of Jesus Christ. No one denies that Jesus lived and died. That's just history. It's the empty tomb and the hundreds of eyewitnesses who saw Jesus after his death that make us scratch our heads. Because science can only prove something that is repeatable, we are dependent upon the eyewitness testimonies of Jesus' resurrection for this once-in-history moment. If Jesus rose from the dead—and I believe he did—Jesus is exactly who he said he was, and he accomplished exactly what had been predicted for thousands of years. He restored us. Jesus made *it*, all of it, right. He can forgive your sins and connect you to the holy God through his life, death, and resurrection.

PART 4: ONE DAY, GOD WILL MAKE ALL THINGS NEW.

The best news is that this is not as good as it gets. A day is coming when Christ will return. He's coming back to re-create our world: a place with no tears, no pain, no suffering, no brokenness, no helplessness—just love. God will make all things new. In the meantime, God invites you to step into his storyline, to join him in his work of restoring all things. Rescued restorers live with purpose and on mission: not a life devoid of hardship, but one filled with enduring hope.

RESPONDING TO GOD'S STORYLINE

If the storyline of Scripture feels like a lightbulb turning on in your soul, that, my friend, is the one true, living God, who eternally exists as Father, Son, and Holy Spirit. God is inviting you into a relationship with him to have your sins forgiven and secure a place in his presence forever. When you locate your story within God's story of redemption, you begin a lifelong relationship with God that brings meaning, hope, and restoration to your life.

Take a moment now to begin a relationship with Christ:

God, I believe the story of the Bible, that Jesus is Lord and you raised him from the dead to forgive my sins and make our relationship possible. Your storyline is now my story. I want to learn how to love you and share your love with others. Amen.

If you confess with your lips that Jesus is Lord and believe in your heart that God raised him from the dead, you will be saved.

ROMANS 10:9

How to Use This Bible Study

THE **STORYLINE BIBLE STUDIES** are versatile and can be used for

- individual study (self-paced),
- small groups (five- or ten-lesson curriculum), or
- church ministry (semester-long curriculum).

INDIVIDUAL STUDY

Each lesson in the *Sticks* Bible study is divided into four fifteen- to twenty-minute parts (sixty to eighty minutes of individual study time per lesson). You can work through the material one part at a time over a few different days or all in one sitting. Either way, this study will be like anything good in your life: What you put in, you get out. Each of the four parts of each lesson will help you practice Bible-study methods.

SMALL GROUPS

Working through the *Sticks* Bible study with a group could be a catalyst for life change. Although the Holy Spirit can teach you truth when you read the Bible on your own, I want to encourage you to gather a small group together to work through this study for these reasons:

- God himself is in communion as one essence and three persons: Father, Son, and Holy Spirit.
- Interconnected, interdependent relationships are hallmarks of the Christian faith life.
- When we collaborate with each other in Bible study, we have access to the viewpoints of our brothers and sisters in Christ, which enrich our understanding of the truth.

For this Bible study, every small-group member will need a copy of the *Sticks* study guide. In addition, I've created a free downloadable small-group guide that includes

- discussion questions for each lesson,
- Scripture readings, and
- prayer prompts.

Whether you've been a discussion leader for decades or just volunteered to lead a group for the first time, you'll find the resources you need to create a loving atmosphere for men and women to grow in Christlikeness. You can download the small-group guide using this QR code.

CHURCH MINISTRY

Church and ministry leaders: Your work is sacred. I know that planning and leading through a semester of ministry can be both challenging and rewarding. That's why every **Storyline Bible Study** is written so that you can build modular semesters of ministry. The *Sticks* Bible study is designed to complement the *Stones*

Bible study. Together, *Sticks* and *Stones* can support a whole semester of ministry seamlessly, inviting the people you lead into God's Word and making your life simpler.

To further equip church and ministry leaders, I've created *The Leader's Guide*, a free digital resource. You can download *The Leader's Guide* using this QR code.

The Leader's Guide offers these resources:

- a sample ministry calendar for a ten-plus-lesson semester of ministry,
- small-group discussion questions for each lesson,
- Scripture readings for each lesson,
- prayer prompts for each lesson,
- five teaching topics for messages that could be taught in large-group settings, and
- resources for deeper study.

SPECIAL FEATURES

However you decide to utilize the *Sticks* Bible study, whether for individual, self-paced devotional time; as a small-group curriculum; or for semester-long church ministry, you'll notice several stand-out features unique to the **Storyline Bible Studies**:

- gospel presentation at the beginning of each Bible study;
- full Scripture passages included in the study so that you can mark up the text and keep your notes in one place;
- insights from diverse scholars, authors, and Bible teachers;
- an emphasis on close readings of large portions of Scripture;
- following one theme instead of focusing on one verse or passage;
- Christological narrative theology without a lot of church-y words; and
- retrospective or imaginative readings of the Bible to help Christians follow the storyline of Scripture.

You may have studied the Bible by book, topic, or passage before; all those approaches are enriching ways to read the Word of God. The **Storyline Bible Studies** follow a literary thread to deepen your appreciation for God's master plan of redemption and develop your skill in connecting the Old Testament to the New.

THE STICKS STORYLINE

Other than God and people, the Bible mentions trees more than any other living thing. There is a tree on the first page of Genesis, in the first psalm, on the first page of the New Testament, and on the last page of Revelation. Every significant theological event in the Bible is marked by a tree.[1]

MATTHEW SLEETH, *REFORESTING FAITH: WHAT TREES TEACH US ABOUT THE NATURE OF GOD AND HIS LOVE FOR US*

ADULTHOOD IS OVERGROWN with a matrix of decision making. Whether it's whom to date, whether to get married, which job to take, which school to send your kids to, or where to live, our decision trees branch out in several directions simultaneously. If I had to guess, I'd bet you're in the middle of making some major life decisions right now. You're not alone—I'm right there with you.

Sometimes the decision tree is overwhelming, with too many options to choose from. Other times, there's an obvious choice, but it requires more effort than I want to give. In these moments of decision fatigue, I want to reach for the low-hanging fruit of autonomy and just do what's easiest—things that seem right in my own eyes.

I don't know about you, but when crucial choices are too daunting or uncertain, I freeze. Meanwhile, new choices just keep popping up in life. It's never-ending.

But Scripture offers us an anchor. What I have found studying trees in the Bible is that God meets us in our decisions and offers us clarity and hope.

Every tree, bush, or vine we survey in this Bible study is deeply embedded in an ancient, symbol-driven world where imagery of a story didn't just matter—it had meaning. Sometimes God repurposes familiar symbols or images to signal deeper significance. The *Sticks* Bible study will guide you through five parts of the Bible where tree imagery is a key element, symbolizing what you and I might call "decision trees." Trees are where God's people go to seek godly wisdom and make hard choices that honor God.

My botanist friends are going to feel as though I stretch the metaphor a bit as I group together Bible stories with trees, a bush, and a vine with branches. As modern readers, we know that trees and bushes and vines are all different plant species. Ancient readers would have been aware of the visual differences too, but I wonder if they connected all the plants, vines, and trees that created firewood or fire sticks together. Based on my word searches and research, there is a thematic connection between all the trees, bushes, and vines we'll study together.[2]

In *Sticks*, we're going to explore these passages:

- *Genesis 2–3*: The Tree of Life and the Tree of the Knowledge of Good and Evil will show us how to choose wisely and not to take matters into our own hands.
- *Exodus 3*: The Burning Bush will help us choose to notice when God is trying to get our attention.
- *Isaiah 1, 6, 11, 53*: The Messiah Tree will help us choose to branch out from our shady family trees.
- *John 15*: The True Vine will teach us how to choose to stay connected to Jesus for a fruitful life.
- *Revelation 22*: The Tree of Life will help us choose to reframe our views from the treetops.

We're going to do this by looking at each story with tree imagery through four different lenses:

- **PART 1: CONTEXT.** Do you ever feel dropped into a Bible story disoriented? Part 1 will introduce you to the passages with tree imagery and help you study those passages in their scriptural context. Getting your bearings before you read will enable you to answer the question *What am I about to read?*

- **PART 2: SEEING.** Do you ever read on autopilot? I do too. Sometimes I finish reading without a clue as to what just happened. A better way to read the Bible is to practice thoughtful, close reading of Scripture to absorb the message God is offering to us. That's why part 2 includes close Scripture reading and observation questions to empower you to answer the question *What is the story saying?*

- **PART 3: UNDERSTANDING.** If you've ever scratched your head after reading your Bible, part 3 will give you the tools to understand the author's intended meaning both for the original audience and for you. Plus you'll practice connecting the Old and New Testaments to get a fuller picture of God's unchanging grace. Part 3 will enable you to answer the question *What does it mean?*

- **PART 4: RESPONDING.** The purpose of Bible study is to help you become more Christlike; that's why part 4 will include journaling space for your reflection on and responses to the content and a blank checklist for actionable next steps. You'll be able to process what you're learning so that you can live out the concepts and pursue Christlikeness. Part 4 will enable you to answer the questions *What truths is this passage teaching?* and *How do I apply this to my life?*

One of my prayers for you, as a curious Bible reader, is that our journey through this study will help you cultivate a biblical imagination so that you're able to make connections throughout the whole storyline of the Bible. In each lesson, I'll do my best to include a few verses from different places in the Bible that are connected to our tree passages. In the course of this study, we'll see the way God shows up in tree imagery throughout his Word—and get a glimpse of how he might show up in our lives today.

God's Word is so wonderful, I hardly know how to contain my excitement. Feel free to geek out with me; let your geek flag fly high, my friends. When we can see how interrelated all the parts of Scripture are to each other, we'll find our affection for God stirred as we see his artistic brilliance unfold.

CHOOSING WISELY INSTEAD OF TAKING MATTERS INTO YOUR OWN HANDS

THE TREE OF LIFE AND THE TREE OF THE KNOWLEDGE OF GOOD AND EVIL: WHERE ADAM AND EVE LISTEN TO THE WRONG VOICE

SCRIPTURE: GENESIS 2–3

PART 1

CONTEXT

Before you begin your study, we will start with the context of the story we are about to read together: the setting, both cultural and historical; the people involved; and where our passage fits in the larger setting of Scripture. All these things help us make sense of what we're reading. Understanding the context of a Bible story is fundamental to reading Scripture well. Getting your bearings before you read will enable you to answer the question *What am I about to read?*

BEAR GRYLLS IS FAMOUS in our house for his harrowing adventures and survival skills. You and I don't know each other well—at least not yet—so I'll tell you now that adventure and survival are not in the realm of my interests. Safety, security, and comfort rank as some of my highest values. But my husband, Aaron, and my son, Caleb? They welcome opportunities to emulate the hero of the *Man vs. Wild* TV show.

Bear Grylls is renowned for

- serving in the British special forces;
- fighting his way back to health after breaking his back in three places during a free-fall parachuting accident;
- being one of the youngest people to scale Mount Everest;

- starring in Emmy-award-nominated TV shows, where he adventures with people like former president Barack Obama; and
- writing over ninety-five books.[1]

The dude's intense. He's kind of like a real-life, wilderness-bound James Bond, foraging for life among the wild. I don't get it. Send me to the beach for some sun and a nap, please. But not Bear Grylls. His insatiable curiosity compels him to explore the wilderness, hunting for adventure.

If I enter my house to the sound of howling laughter or roaring *ah*s, I know Aaron and Caleb are glued to a Bear Grylls TV show. One time, Caleb explained that Bear was trying to decide if he wanted to eat raw bird eggs for sustenance or risk digesting the berries excreted in bear poop. My usual response to this kind of commentary is "Why, though? Just why?" Caleb will say, "Because it's awesome, Mommy!"

In a desperate attempt to involve me in a Bear Grylls adventure, Caleb asked me to imagine knowing what Bear knows. If I could navigate the wilderness, he suggested—if I were wise to the animal kingdom, if Mother Nature and I were besties—I wouldn't just love what Bear Grylls accomplished, I'd try it for myself. The innocence of children is a precious thing. I didn't want to put a damper on my son's dream, so I simply responded with a "Maybe."

If you take my resistance out of the equation, my son's reasoning is sound. Knowing how to navigate the wilderness would make it fun, *potentially*. Bear knows the lay of the land anywhere he goes. He knows which plants to eat and not, which animals to hunt and not, which terrain is safe and not. All his wise choices are founded on awareness and understanding of what will be good for him and what will be bad.

I have zero desire to emulate Bear's adventures, but I'd love to have as much knowledge and confidence as he does when he makes his decisions in the wilderness. I want to navigate my life with wisdom—knowing what is good for me and what is not.

Here's what I want to suggest to you: The Bible has a whole lot to teach us about discernment. You and I can't treat the Bible like our personal decision-making handbook, but we can seek God's wisdom in the Scriptures. And when we do, we'll find that God is inviting us to learn from him and his people.

We are about to enter the wild world that is the Torah, or the first five books of the Bible. Here we will see the first of many mentions of tree imagery in the Scriptures. Trees planted by God, our Cosmic Gardener, sprout from verses from the beginning of the Bible to the end, growing to provide life's necessities. But two central trees begin the storyline of Scripture: the Tree of Life and the Tree of the Knowledge of Good and Evil.

Embedded in the Genesis Creation narratives are verses we can use to shape our theology of sin and humanity, our understanding of humanity's origin, and many other important subjects. As Reverend Fleming Rutledge would say, "its depths are inexhaustible."[2] But in our study together, we're focusing on one particular goal: how the Tree of Life and the Tree of the Knowledge of Good and Evil can function as literary devices—a thread in the storyline of Scripture.

Navigating the Garden of Eden as Western, modern Christians presents real challenges, so before we dive in, let's get a bird's-eye view. The Torah was written and edited by Moses to create a single, unified story with an overarching message: "God's relationship with his people has a future, even though they have proven faithless in the past."[3] Yes, and amen.

It's important to remember that *although the Bible is for us, it was not written to us.* Moses had a specific audience in mind when he wrote Genesis, Exodus, Leviticus, Numbers, and Deuteronomy: the Israelites who were about to enter the Promised Land.[4] The Patriarchs—Abraham, Isaac, Jacob, Joseph—had all passed away. The escape from Egypt, through the Red Sea, was in the distant past. As they emerged from the wilderness, Moses' audience faced a critical choice: Would they follow God, or would they repeat the unfaithfulness of generations past? They were on the

> The garden is an act of utter graciousness. But the trees disclose the character of that graciousness. There is no cheap grace here.[5]
>
> Walter Brueggemann, *Genesis: A Bible Commentary for Teaching and Preaching*

precipice of the land God promised—but could they, would they, choose wisely and actually reach it?

Moses begins the Torah with God's creative activity: breathing the world into order and breathing life into his image bearers. The Creator exhorted Adam and Eve to enjoy all the trees in the Garden, even the Tree of Life. But there was one limitation: They were not to eat the fruit of the Tree of the Knowledge of Good and Evil.

It's God's garden and God's covenant with Adam and Eve, so he gets to set the terms. Do you bristle at that? I know I do. My Western culture encourages me to be self-sufficient and independent, without limitations. Good or bad, those are some of the messages I'm consuming on a regular basis, and they've shaped me, whether I like to admit it or not. That's why living on God's terms can be a challenge.

But your limitations, and mine, were designed by our Creator in love. I know as soon as I mention our limitations, some of us are already problem-solving our finitude. But taking matters into our own hands is not going to lead to flourishing lives. Adam and Eve will show us that much is true.

Embracing that God knows best *and* has our best in mind is a truth I hope takes root in our souls through this lesson. We don't have to have all the answers to make wise choices—we need to trust God's wisdom and wait on him to dispense wisdom to us as we come to him with our questions, seek out wise counsel, and search the Scriptures for guidance.

As we follow the tree line and zoom in on the Garden of Eden, Moses will teach us about ourselves, our world, and the human condition through the tale of two trees.

You're going to see in this lesson that taking matters into our own hands is not going to lead to flourishing lives.

The qualities in the Garden of Eden put human nature to a test.[6]

Terje Stordalen, *Echoes of Eden*

1. **PERSONAL CONTEXT: What is going on in your life right now that might impact how you understand this Bible story?**

2. **SPIRITUAL CONTEXT: If you've never studied this Bible story before, what piques your curiosity? If you've studied this passage before, what impressions and insights do you recall? What problems or concerns might you have with the passage?**

SEEING

Seeing the text is vital if we want the heart of the Scripture passage to sink in. We read slowly and intentionally through the text with the context in mind. As we practice close, thoughtful reading of Scripture, we pick up on phrases, implications, and meanings we might otherwise have missed. Part 2 includes close Scripture reading and observation questions to empower you to answer the question *What is the story saying?*

1. **Read Genesis 2:4-17 and draw a triangle around each mention of a tree.**

⁴ This is the account of the heavens and the earth when they were created, when the LORD God made the earth and the heavens.

⁵ Now no shrub had yet appeared on the earth and no plant had yet sprung up, for the LORD God had not sent rain on the earth and there was no one to work the ground, ⁶ but streams came up from the earth and watered the whole surface of the ground. ⁷ Then the LORD God formed a man from the dust of the ground and breathed into his nostrils the breath of life, and the man became a living being.

⁸ Now the LORD God had planted a garden in the east, in Eden; and there he put the man he had formed. ⁹ The LORD God made all kinds of trees grow out of the ground—trees that were pleasing to the eye and good for food. In

the middle of the garden were the tree of life and the tree of the knowledge of good and evil.

¹⁰ A river watering the garden flowed from Eden; from there it was separated into four headwaters. ¹¹ The name of the first is the Pishon; it winds through the entire land of Havilah, where there is gold. ¹² (The gold of that land is good; aromatic resin and onyx are also there.) ¹³ The name of the second river is the Gihon; it winds through the entire land of Cush. ¹⁴ The name of the third river is the Tigris; it runs along the east side of Ashur. And the fourth river is the Euphrates.

¹⁵ The LORD God took the man and put him in the Garden of Eden to work it and take care of it. ¹⁶ And the LORD God commanded the man, "You are free to eat from any tree in the garden; ¹⁷ but you must not eat from the tree of the knowledge of good and evil, for when you eat from it you will certainly die."

GENESIS 2:4–17, NIV

2. Based on Genesis 2:9, where was the Tree of Life located in the Garden of Eden?

☐ east of the Garden

☐ on the west side of the Garden

☐ in the middle of the Garden

The Tree of Life represents the good life—when you are living in harmony with God.[7] And it also represents eternal life—life beyond the life God breathed into the world and into humanity. If Adam and Eve had continued to eat the fruit of the Tree of Life, they would have lived forever. Smack dab in the middle of the Garden, God placed a self-sustaining tree, the fruit of which kept them

The tree of life is a supreme image at once of edenic splendor and of paradise lost—an image of nostalgia and longing for a lost perfection.[8]

Leland Ryken, James C. Wilhoit, and Tremper Longman III, eds., *Dictionary of Biblical Imagery*

from being subject to death. Before Adam and Eve drew their first breath, they had everything they needed for a fruitful, flourishing, beautiful life. Theologically speaking, this sets the stage for a core truth of Christianity: *Eternal life is something we receive, not something we earn.*

3. **Write out what God said about the trees in the Garden in Genesis 2:16-17. Understanding his exact words will be important because the serpent manipulates God's words later in the story.**

66

99

4. **What does God say will be the consequence of eating the fruit of the Tree of the Knowledge of Good and Evil (Genesis 2:17)? Check the right answer.**

   ☐ He would kill Adam and Eve.

   ☐ They would die.

Studying Genesis 2 and 3 at this point in my life exposed a lot of negative assumptions I've made about our good God. I think I'd had it in my mind that God threatened to kill Adam and Eve himself, but that is *not* what he says. God clearly communicates the natural consequence of eating from the Tree of the Knowledge of Good and Evil: Adam and Eve would be subject to death. In contrast, the Tree of Life would provide a forever future in God's goodness and wisdom.

5. **Read Genesis 3:1-24 and draw a triangle around every mention of a tree.**

   3 Now the serpent was more crafty than any of the wild animals the LORD God had made. He said to the woman, "Did God really say, 'You must not eat from any tree in the garden'?"

   ² The woman said to the serpent, "We may eat fruit from the trees

in the garden, ³ but God did say, 'You must not eat fruit from the tree that is in the middle of the garden, and you must not touch it, or you will die.'"

⁴ "You will not certainly die," the serpent said to the woman. ⁵ "For God knows that when you eat from it your eyes will be opened, and you will be like God, knowing good and evil."

⁶ When the woman saw that the fruit of the tree was good for food and pleasing to the eye, and also desirable for gaining wisdom, she took some and ate it. She also gave some to her husband, who was with her, and he ate it. ⁷ Then the eyes of both of them were opened, and they realized they were naked; so they sewed fig leaves together and made coverings for themselves.

⁸ Then the man and his wife heard the sound of the LORD God as he was walking in the garden in the cool of the day, and they hid from the LORD God among the trees of the garden. ⁹ But the LORD God called to the man, "Where are you?"

¹⁰ He answered, "I heard you in the garden, and I was afraid because I was naked; so I hid."

¹¹ And he said, "Who told you that you were naked? Have you eaten from the tree that I commanded you not to eat from?"

¹² The man said, "The woman you put here with me—she gave me some fruit from the tree, and I ate it."

¹³ Then the LORD God said to the woman, "What is this you have done?"

The woman said, "The serpent deceived me, and I ate."

¹⁴ So the LORD God said to the serpent, "Because you have done this,

"Cursed are you above all livestock
	and all wild animals!
You will crawl on your belly
	and you will eat dust
	all the days of your life.
¹⁵ And I will put enmity

between you and the woman,
and between your offspring and hers;
he will crush your head,
and you will strike his heel."

¹⁶ To the woman he said,

"I will make your pains in childbearing very severe;
with painful labor you will give birth to children.
Your desire will be for your husband,
and he will rule over you."

¹⁷ To Adam he said, "Because you listened to your wife and ate fruit from the tree about which I commanded you, 'You must not eat from it,'

"Cursed is the ground because of you;
through painful toil you will eat food from it
all the days of your life.
¹⁸ It will produce thorns and thistles for you,
and you will eat the plants of the field.
¹⁹ By the sweat of your brow
you will eat your food
until you return to the ground,
since from it you were taken;
for dust you are
and to dust you will return."

²⁰ Adam named his wife Eve, because she would become the mother of all the living.
²¹ The LORD God made garments of skin for Adam and his wife and clothed them. ²² And the LORD God said, "The man has now become like one of us, knowing good and evil. He must not be allowed to reach out his

hand and take also from the tree of life and eat, and live forever." [23] So the LORD God banished him from the Garden of Eden to work the ground from which he had been taken. [24] After he drove the man out, he placed on the east side of the Garden of Eden cherubim and a flaming sword flashing back and forth to guard the way to the tree of life.

GENESIS 3:1-24, NIV

6. **Reread Genesis 2:9 and check all that apply to all the trees in the Garden.**

    ☐ pleasing to the eye

    ☐ good for food

    ☐ exactly what Eve needed

7. **Reread Genesis 3:6 and check all that apply. Eve viewed the Tree of the Knowledge of Good and Evil as . . .**

    ☐ pleasing to the eye

    ☐ good for food

    ☐ the only meal available

    ☐ desirable for gaining wisdom

Notice the similarities and difference between God's view of the trees in the Garden and Eve's. The distinction reveals where Eve went wrong. After her conversation with the serpent, she started to believe that to gain wisdom, she needed the fruit from the Tree of the Knowledge of Good and Evil. But consider—who is the Source of wisdom? The very God who walked in the Garden with Adam and Eve every day. Maybe the choice before Eve (and Adam), as they walked past

[God] wanted them to follow his command not to eat their fruit and to accept that his plans were far wiser than theirs. Disobedience would show that they foolishly prized independence more than a relationship with God.[9]

Jesudason Baskar Jeyaraj, "Genesis," in *South Asia Bible Commentary*

both trees each day, was more about *how, where, and from whom they would seek wisdom*. Would they mature into wisdom through deepening relationship with and connection to God, or would they try to acquire wisdom by themselves, grabbing at the low-hanging fruit of the Tree of the Knowledge of Good and Evil?

8. **Reread Genesis 3:3. Where was the Tree of the Knowledge of Good and Evil?**

   ☐ east of the Garden

   ☐ on the west side of the Garden

   ☐ in the middle of the Garden

At the center of the Garden, the Tree of the Knowledge of Good and Evil stood alongside the Tree of Life. But in stark contrast to the Tree of Life—a picture of a maturing, unending life sustained by God's presence—the Tree of the Knowledge of Good and Evil represents autonomy, doing life on your own.

The pairing embodies what you and I know to be true in our own experience. When we have to make a hard choice, it's usually in the middle of a tough situation. And side by side in that tough situation are two choices: the life-giving way of God and the death-dealing decision to go it alone. To choose life, we must reject the temptations keeping us from enjoying God's goodness. When we're faced with an enemy, we can make a conscious decision to love that person, or we can choose to match their vitriol. When circumstances are exasperating, we can choose to be patient and seek God's guidance, or we can choose to power forward in our own strength.

9. **What happened as soon as Adam and Eve ate the fruit of the Tree of the Knowledge of Good and Evil? Check all that apply.**

   ☐ Their eyes were opened.

   ☐ They knew they were naked.

   ☐ They died.

Before rejecting God's instructions, Adam and Eve were not aware of their vulnerabilities in the Garden of Eden. According to the creators of BibleProject, Tim

Mackie and Jon Collins,[11] the Garden scene described the innocence Adam and Eve maintained before the Fall. They were in an infant stage of maturity because they were in the beginning stages of their relationship with God. Not tasting the fruit of the Tree of the Knowledge of Good and Evil meant Adam and Eve were free to gain wisdom through God's presence. But when they chose their own way, their eyes were opened—they were naked and unable to survive apart from God's care. Wisdom, too, would be harder to find—because they had separated themselves from the One who gives it.

PART 3

UNDERSTANDING

Now that we've finished a close reading of the Scriptures, we're going to spend some time on interpretation: doing our best to understand what God was saying to the original audience and what he's teaching us through the process. But to do so, we need to learn his ways and consider how God's Word would have been understood by the original audience before applying the same truths to our own lives. "Scripture interpretation" may sound a little stuffy, but understanding what God means to communicate to us in the Bible is crucial to enjoying a close relationship with Jesus. Part 3 will enable you to answer the question *What does it mean?*

THE ARTISTRY OF GOD'S STORYTELLING amazes me. The Genesis story begins with God placing Adam and Eve in paradise alongside two trees in the middle of the Garden of Eden. Maybe Adam and Eve had walked by those trees every day of their whole lives. Maybe that's where God had met them for their walks to dispense wisdom. But now, after Adam and Eve have refused to trust God's instructions, the two trees are where shame tries to hide. The trees have exposed Adam and Eve's vulnerabilities, and now the man and woman hope the trees can hide those same vulnerabilities. This sounds like nonsense, right? The trees can't both expose you and hide you. But in my own life, I test this concept time and time again.

If humanity would simply acknowledge the innate authority of the Creator, would recognize that they were tenants and stewards in God's garden, they would live in paradise forever. But . . . if they had to be *autonomous* of the authority of the great King, then they would die. . . . The choice was autonomy.[12]

Sandra L. Richter, *The Epic of Eden*

1. List the three questions God asks Adam and Eve in Genesis 3:9–11:

1.

2.

3.

There's a graciousness in asking questions. God does not yell. He does not point fingers. He does not explode with anger or denigrate Adam and Eve's reach for wisdom. He asks hard questions. My educator friends tell me this is one of the most effective ways to help children own up to their mistakes, experience accountability, and process how to make better decisions. If we consider Adam and Eve as moral infants, we see the kindness, the gentleness, in God's reaction.

My heart sinks at this point in the story. Absent from Adam and Eve's response to the Lord is confession, repentance, or a willingness to change. And this reaction hits a little too close to home, doesn't it? When I read the Bible, I relate most to the hardheaded, unfaithful impulses of the main characters. That instinct to dig in, to throw up defenses, to go it alone—I imagine a lot of us know how that feels. As Adam and Eve squirm before God's questions, wedged between the Tree of Life and the Tree of the Knowledge of Good and Evil . . . well, if we're honest, we can picture ourselves there too.

2. **Notice with me the mercy of God after he explains the consequences of their foolishness. Write the last thing God says in the story before Adam and Eve are exiled from Eden (Genesis 3:22):**

"

"

3. **Based on Genesis 3:22, what is God's main concern regarding Adam and Eve now that they have chosen to grab wisdom never intended for them?**

   ☐ They will compete with God.

   ☐ They will try and take over.

   ☐ They will live forever.

Now that Adam and Eve will experience evil, God mercifully restricts their access to the Tree of Life to keep them from experiencing evil *forever*. Being excluded from God's paradise is a crushing consequence, but the motivation behind it shows that God always is and always will be loving. Even when we mess up big time.

MAKING CONNECTIONS

An important part of understanding the meaning of a Bible passage is getting a sense of its place in the broader storyline of Scripture. When we make connections between different parts of the Bible, we get a glimpse of the unity and cohesion of the Scriptures.

Adam and Eve's story under the two trees points us to a larger theme in Scripture: that *our fundamental sin, the thing that keeps us separated from God, is trying to take for ourselves what only God can give.* In fact, Moses shapes his book in the editorial process to repeat that theme: Throughout Genesis, people take and give things they should only receive from God, and they experience the consequences of that choice. Dru Johnson's book *The Universal Story* helped me see this thread in Genesis clearly (I practically have the entirety of that book underlined or highlighted).[13]

Let's take a look at some of the other passages in Genesis that color in the theme first outlined in Adam and Eve's story:

SOME BIBLICAL EXAMPLES OF HUMANS TAKING WHAT ONLY GOD CAN GIVE

Eve	Genesis 3:6, 17	Eve takes and gives the fruit of the Tree of the Knowledge of Good and Evil to Adam, and God's curse to the man has to do with him listening to the voice of his wife.
Sarai (Sarah)	Genesis 16:1-3	Sarai takes and gives her servant Hagar to Abram, who listened to her voice.
Rebekah	Genesis 27:8, 15-17	Rebekah takes and gives Esau's clothing and stew to Jacob and tells Jacob to listen to her voice.

4. What similarities do you notice between these three stories? What differences?

The disobedience of the man and woman is depicted not so much as an act of great wickedness or a great transgression as an act of great folly. They had all the "good" they would have needed, but they wanted more—they wanted to be like God.[14]

John H. Sailhamer, *The Pentateuch as Narrative*

5. Why do you think these women were tempted to take matters into their own hands?

6. In each of these stories, what were the implications and consequences of taking and giving things we should only receive from God?

We need to be careful not to reduce Adam and Eve's failure to a battle of the sexes, or assume that because these other stories feature women that this all boils down to gender roles. Many Bible students and teachers have sought to discredit women—all women—because of women's failures in the Scriptures, but if we look at the whole of Scripture, the pattern in both men and women involves listening to the wrong voice. That's what really went wrong in the Garden of Eden: Eve *and Adam* listened to the wrong voice, the voice of the serpent.

7. Describe one situation in your own life where you are tempted to take or receive something you should only be getting from God. What voice are you listening to? What choices would help you listen to God's voice instead?

My family and I made a decision very recently that confused a lot of people in our life. Those closest to us completely understood our reasoning and celebrated our act of obedience. But we still get questions about why we chose to go this route and lots of unsolicited advice encouraging us to consider the alternative.

I have been tempted time and time again to reevaluate whether I made the right choice because I have a lot of practice taking matters into my own hands. At the end of the day, I know, and my family knows, that the decision we made together was the wise one.

If you are at a crossroads now, I am praying the rest of this lesson brings you some peace and clarity. Rarely do our decisions come without some ambiguity, but I can tell you this: *If you can resist the urge to listen to voices that do not align with God's truth, you'll be better positioned to receive the best God has for you.*

— — —

In every lesson we'll expand our storyline chart to include all the tree imagery we're studying together.

THE STICKS STORYLINE OF SCRIPTURE

Stick(s)	Element of Fire	The Decision
the Tree of Life & the Tree of the Knowledge of Good and Evil (Genesis 2–3)	Flaming swords of the cherubim guard the Garden of Eden after the exile.	Will we choose to live wisely with wisdom from God or try to take matters into our own hands?
the Burning Bush (Exodus 3)	The Sinai tree/bush is in flames but is not consumed.	Will we take notice when God is trying get our attention or ignore his voice and keep moving on?
the Messiah Tree (Isaiah 1, 6, 11, 53)	The smoke in the Temple and the flaming coals burn with heat from the fire.	Will we branch out from our shady family trees and grow deep roots in God's family?
the True Vine, Jesus (John 15)	The branches who do not abide in Jesus wither and are used as firewood.	Will we stay connected to Jesus for a fruitful life or try to produce good fruit on our own?
the Tree of Life (Revelation 22)	If you choose to live outside the Garden City gates, you will be cast into a lake of fire.	Will we choose to reframe our perspective or follow old patterns?

Fear Response	Consequences of the Wrong Choice	Wise Choice
Adam and Eve hide from God between the trees out of fear and shame.	When Adam and Eve choose to seek wisdom for themselves, they end up exiled from Eden.	Trust God to give us wisdom through an ongoing relationship with him.
Moses hides his face from God at the Burning Bush out of fear.	If the Israelites don't choose to follow Moses in the Exodus, they will remain in Egypt as slaves and exiles.	Notice, listen to, and trust God's voice when he's trying to get our attention.
The prophet Isaiah asks God how long his judgment will last, fearing none will survive.	Since the Israelites choose idolatry, God allows them to be exiled from Jerusalem and enslaved to the Babylonians and Assyrians.	Remain faithful to God, knowing he's always going to be faithful to us.
Jesus quickly encourages his followers that his friendship and love for them does not waver, as if he knows his words will cause fear.	Those who do not choose to abide in Christ will be exiled to fire, where all efforts will be consumed and reduced to ashes.	Stay close to Jesus to bear good fruit.
There will be no more fear in the new heaven and new earth.	If we do not choose to follow Christ, the Tree of Life, we will be exiled to the lake of fire.	Choose to live near the Tree of Life.

1. What choice are you facing right now? How can you pay attention to where God is at work?

2. What did you learn about God's character in this lesson?

3. How should these truths shape your faith community and change you?

RESPONDING

The purpose of Bible study is to help you become more Christlike; that's why part 4 will include journaling space for your reflection on and responses to the content and a blank checklist for actionable next steps. You'll be able to process what you're learning so that you can live out the concepts and pursue Christlikeness. Part 4 will enable you to answer the questions *What truths is this passage teaching?* and *How do I apply this to my life?*

ADAM AND EVE FACED A DECISION with massive implications. Would they live on the fruit of the Tree of Life or take the forbidden fruit of the Tree of the Knowledge of Good and Evil? Theologically speaking, we have the same choice: We can live on the fruit of the Tree of Life—which represents God's righteousness—or we can pick the fruit of the Tree of the Knowledge of Good and Evil, taking righteousness into our own hands. *The tree we choose determines the fruit we will bear.* Will we choose wisely, or take what seems to be the easier road? A few truths will help us understand the weightiness of our decision:

1. WISDOM ISN'T UP FOR GRABS; IT'S A GIFT FROM YOUR CREATOR.
Throughout the Old Testament and the New, the Bible repeats a concept so often it's obvious that every generation has needed the reminder: *We must not be wise in our own eyes.*

- The book of Proverbs says not to be wise in our own eyes (Proverbs 3:7).
- Isaiah warns his audience sternly: "Woe" to those who think they are wise (Isaiah 5:21, NIV).
- The apostle Paul echoes the sentiment in the book of Romans when he repeats the same thing: Do not be wise in your own eyes (Romans 12:16).

Apparently, this is a universal human problem: We think we know better than God. The book of the Bible that illustrates this probably most overtly—and, might I add, gruesomely—is Judges. Repeated in the book of Judges is that phrase once again: The people were doing what seemed right in their own eyes. And what's the fallout of living that way? The book shows us a dumpster fire of human depravity. It's a powerful warning: *Wisdom is not up for grabs; wisdom always originates in God.*

The next time you want to seize the moment or get ahead of God's leading, remember the life-giving words of Proverbs 3:5: "Trust in the Lord with all your heart and lean not on your own understanding" (NIV). And be encouraged: Wisdom isn't up for grabs, but our good God wants nothing more than to gift you his own wisdom.

But, thanks be to God, this is not the end of the story. They did not die in the day they ate of the tree. . . . Instead, an animal died so that God could make garments of skin to cover their nakedness (3:21). The innocent died instead of the guilty; substitutionary atonement through the shedding of blood is the only way that an unrighteous person can be made righteous (Heb. 9:22).[15]

Glenn Kreider, *Vindicating the Vixens*

---

2. IF YOU LACK WISDOM, ASK GOD FOR MORE.

Have you ever found yourself in a situation that goes way beyond your experience or education? I know I have.

- I started a nonprofit in my twenties, long before I knew what I was doing. While the nonprofit continues to mature into a national organization fifteen years later, I find myself regularly begging God to guide us because I still feel unprepared to lead.

- I know what it is to talk to a nurse about removing care from a parent. I wouldn't wish this on my worst enemy. No one readies you for that kind of heartache.

- I'm balancing ministry life as a Bible teacher while also serving as a pastor's wife. Honoring both roles is a work in progress.

As my story unfolds, I'm more acutely aware of how very little wisdom I possess. Your own life experiences are different from mine, but undoubtedly, you've found yourself navigating choices that are simply beyond your own wisdom. That's okay. It really is. Lacking wisdom is not a reflection of your love for God—it just means you're human and you need God. The good news is that God promises Christ followers he will give us wisdom when we ask for it (James 1:5, NLT): "If you need wisdom, ask our generous God, and he will give it to you. He will not rebuke you for asking." If you find yourself out of your depth, don't go it alone: Ask God for the wisdom you need.

3. UNWISE CHOICES DON'T CANCEL YOUR FUTURE.

I feel like I have a PhD in messing things up. Whether it's sticking my foot in my mouth or letting my anger control me, I've got plenty of experience in missing the mark. I also know what it feels like to be frozen, overwhelmed by a flowchart of possibilities. In both situations, I tend to act unwisely.

What naturally follows my unwise choices? Shame—lots of it. I imagine how utterly impossible a bright future will be now that I've derailed God's plans.

I wonder if that's how Adam and Eve felt as they hid behind the Tree of the Knowledge of Good and Evil. That's why it's vital for us to remember: *God's good plans for Adam and Eve were not canceled because of their unwise choices.* Yes, they experienced consequences—severe ones. But as my friend Glenn Kreider says, "Thanks be to God, this is not the end of the story." If you've made some unwise choices lately, or you're obsessing over some unwise choices in your past, accept God's grace for you. Your unwise choices have not canceled your future. Your future is full of hope in Christ.

Use this journaling space to process what you are learning.

Ask yourself how these truths impact your relationship with God and with others.

What is the Holy Spirit bringing to your mind as actionable next steps in your faith journey?

-

-

-

TAKING NOTICE WHEN GOD IS TRYING TO GET YOUR ATTENTION

THE BURNING BUSH:
WHERE GOD REVEALS HIS IDENTITY TO MOSES

SCRIPTURE: EXODUS 3

PART 1

CONTEXT

Before you begin your study, we will start with the context of the story we are about to read together: the setting, both cultural and historical; the people involved; and where our passage fits in the larger setting of Scripture. All these things help us make sense of what we're reading. Understanding the context of a Bible story is fundamental to reading Scripture well. Getting your bearings before you read will enable you to answer the question *What am I about to read?*

I DIDN'T GROW UP cheering for Aggie football. Our family was into tennis—Pete Sampras, to be exact. But my freshman year at Texas A&M left me slack-jawed at the intensity of Aggie pride. I wanted to immerse myself in all Aggieland tradition, and I was most looking forward to experiencing Bonfire, a massive stack of flaming logs that symbolize the burning Aggie desire to beat the University of Texas in football.[1] Tens of thousands of football fans enjoyed Bonfire each year, and I wanted to see the spectacle, to feel the heat myself—if nothing else, to honor the hard work of the students building the Bonfire.

Tragically, Bonfire collapsed in the wee hours of the morning on November 18, 1999. The fall killed twelve people and injured many others. Within hours of the emergency, the entire campus was awake. We were glued to our TVs, watching the news, hushed by the collective grief spreading across campus like a wildfire. Over twenty years later, the television images of the bonfire cracking are still seared into my brain.

At the base of Mount Horeb (also known as Sinai—19:11), Moses encounters an unquenchable burning bush while herding sheep in the wilderness. The fiery bush is an icon of the Divine. The burning bush expresses both God's merciful accommodation, coming down from the mountain of God to meet Moses, and God's awesome holiness, the unquenchable fire being both dangerous and attractive at the same time.[2]

Dennis T. Olson, "Exodus," in *Theological Bible Commentary*

The university installed a memorial near the front of the campus to honor the victims. I've visited College Station several times lately, and the Bonfire Memorial catches my attention every time—it is so conspicuous and out of the ordinary. You can't drive by it without sensing that you are near holy ground.

As I studied Moses' experience at the Burning Bush, Bonfire struck a match in my imagination. Moses got close enough to God's presence at the Burning Bush that the heat from the burning tree would have warmed his skin, the flames of God illuminating and brightening his face. Like Bonfire and the Bonfire Memorial, Moses' encounter with God is not something we can snuff out of our memory.

In our last lesson, we zoomed in on the first few chapters of the Bible to survey the Eden tree line, and now we are jumping about fifty chapters later into a new book of the Bible. The storyline of trees has deep roots throughout Genesis and into the book of Exodus. When Adam and Eve left Eden, the Garden and its trees were being guarded by flaming cherubim. When Noah constructed the ark, he cut down a lot of trees. How did Noah know the Flood had finally receded? Through a sign, a branch from an olive tree. When Abraham prepared to sacrifice Isaac, he chopped trees to prepare fire sticks. A whole lot of years, trees, and dramatic family history are in the books by the time we get to Moses' story.

Moses' birth signals the miraculous ways God had set his life apart. Moses was born into slavery, and into a moment when the pharaoh of Egypt had issued an edict to kill all the firstborn Hebrew baby boys. Moses escaped the genocide only because of several brave women in his life. First, God-fearing midwives refused to kill baby boys after delivery. Then, his mother built a little mini ark of her own, sailing Moses in a basket down the Nile River. Moses' sister, Miriam, watched over him as he floated until the princess of Egypt came out of the palace, found Moses in the basket, and kept him as her own child. You get the sense that nothing could keep this special baby from fulfilling his calling to emancipate God's people—and the women in his life were mission critical.

As the adopted son of Pharaoh's daughter, Moses enjoyed the privileges of royalty, but he also saw the ruthless injustices the Israelites were suffering under Pharaoh's rule. One particular act of cruelty set Moses off, and he murdered an Egyptian who was beating up a Hebrew slave. Moses fled the palace and left Egypt to escape punishment in Midian.

While Moses fled to Midian, God's people continued to suffer. The pharaoh was a relentless production manager who used an exploitative labor system to keep the Israelites enslaved. Under Pharaoh's oppression, God's people were no longer celebrated as beloved by their Creator; they were treated like expendable commodities to be exploited.

Thankfully, God heard the cries of his weary people and recruited Moses to rescue them through something the Bible calls "the Exodus." The greatest act of salvation in the Old Testament, the Exodus would essentially become "the paradigm for future deliverances" in the Scriptures.[3] But before Moses leads the

God often uses trees when calling his people. In Scripture God called to Gideon (Judges 6:11), Nathanael (John 1:48), and Zacchaeus (Luke 19:1–6) with, through, and in trees. Joan of Arc heard God speak to her when she was in her father's garden. Augustine spoke of hearing the voice of a child while sitting under a fig tree. Martin Luther met God when Luther sought shelter under a tree during a violent thunderstorm.[4]

Matthew Sleeth, *Reforesting Faith*

people out of Egypt, he experiences God's power and presence for himself—at the Burning Bush.

What you are about to read is the story of Moses noticing a burning tree. That's when God reveals himself to Moses and launches a rescue plan for the Israelites to escape the pharaoh's tyranny.

You're going to see that taking notice when God is trying to get our attention is the wisest choice we could possibly make.

1. **PERSONAL CONTEXT: What is going on in your life right now that might impact how you understand this Bible story?**

2. **SPIRITUAL CONTEXT: If you've never studied this Bible story before, what piques your curiosity? If you've studied this passage before, what impressions and insights do you recall? What problems or concerns might you have with the passage?**

SEEING

Seeing the text is vital if we want the heart of the Scripture passage to sink in. We read slowly and intentionally through the text with the context in mind. As we practice close, thoughtful reading of Scripture, we pick up on phrases, implications, and meanings we might otherwise have missed. Part 2 includes close Scripture reading and observation questions to empower you to answer the question *What is the story saying?*

1. **Read Exodus 3:1–18 and underline every time God speaks.**

3 Moses was keeping the flock of his father-in-law Jethro, the priest of Midian; he led his flock beyond the wilderness, and came to Horeb, the mountain of God. ² There the angel of the LORD appeared to him in a flame of fire out of a bush; he looked, and the bush was blazing, yet it was not consumed. ³ Then Moses said, "I must turn aside and look at this great sight, and see why the bush is not burned up." ⁴ When the LORD saw that he had turned aside to see, God called to him out of the bush, "Moses, Moses!" And he said, "Here I am." ⁵ Then he said, "Come no closer! Remove the sandals from your feet, for the place on which you are standing is holy ground." ⁶ He said further, "I am the God of your father, the God of Abraham, the God of Isaac, and the God of Jacob." And

Moses hid his face, for he was afraid to look at God. [7] Then the LORD said, "I have observed the misery of my people who are in Egypt; I have heard their cry on account of their taskmasters. Indeed, I know their sufferings, [8] and I have come down to deliver them from the Egyptians, and to bring them up out of that land to a good and broad land, a land flowing with milk and honey, to the country of the Canaanites, the Hittites, the Amorites, the Perizzites, the Hivites, and the Jebusites. [9] The cry of the Israelites has now come to me; I have also seen how the Egyptians oppress them. [10] So come, I will send you to Pharaoh to bring my people, the Israelites, out of Egypt." [11] But Moses said to God, "Who am I that I should go to Pharaoh, and bring the Israelites out of Egypt?" [12] He said, "I will be with you; and this shall be the sign for you that it is I who sent you: when you have brought the people out of Egypt, you shall worship God on this mountain."

[13] But Moses said to God, "If I come to the Israelites and say to them, 'The God of your ancestors has sent me to you,' and they ask me, 'What is his name?' what shall I say to them?" [14] God said to Moses, "I AM WHO I AM." He said further, "Thus you shall say to the Israelites, 'I AM has sent me to you.'" [15] God also said to Moses, "Thus you shall say to the Israelites, 'The LORD, the God of your ancestors, the God of Abraham, the God of Isaac, and the God of Jacob, has sent me to you':

This is my name forever,
and this my title for all generations.

[16] Go and assemble the elders of Israel, and say to them, 'The LORD, the God of your ancestors, the God of Abraham, of Isaac, and of Jacob, has appeared to me, saying: I have given heed to you and to what has been done to you in Egypt. [17] I declare that I will bring you up out of the

> Moses had probably seen bushes burning in the desert many times before. But he is curious about this one because it does not burn up and turn into ash. So he goes to have a closer look.[5]
>
> P. G. George and Paul Swarup, "Exodus," in *South Asia Bible Commentary*

misery of Egypt, to the land of the Canaanites, the Hittites, the Amorites, the Perizzites, the Hivites, and the Jebusites, a land flowing with milk and honey.' ¹⁸ They will listen to your voice; and you and the elders of Israel shall go to the king of Egypt and say to him, 'The LORD, the God of the Hebrews, has met with us; let us now go a three days' journey into the wilderness, so that we may sacrifice to the LORD our God.'"

EXODUS 3:1-18

2. **According to Exodus 3:2, what caught Moses' attention?**

   ☐ that a bush was burning

   ☐ that a bush was aflame but not consumed

3. **God could have revealed himself to Moses at any time, but according to Exodus 3:4, when did God decide to call out to Moses?**

   ☐ when Moses was ready

   ☐ when Moses sought out God

   ☐ when Moses turned to see why the bush was not burned up

Moses' curiosity seems to be the hinge point in the story. I don't want to make too much of this point, but I also don't want to underestimate God's intentionality in including this detail in the record of Scripture. God waited until Moses got curious—and only *after* Moses turned his body and mind to explore what was happening around him did God choose to reveal who he is and what he was about to do. There may be a message in this to all of us. *Some of our most important moments with God are a combination of God's willingness to disclose himself to us and*

What is remarkable in this case is the way the angel appears: as a flame of fire in a bush. The bush is blazing. It looks as though it is on fire, but the fire does not consume it. There is nothing at all like this in the rest of the Bible. It is a unique form of theophany.[6]

Richard Bauckham, *Who Is God?*

---

our ability to take notice when he is already at work. Moses could have carried on with his flock of sheep, but he rerouted to follow unusual activity.

4. According to Exodus 3:6, how does God identify himself to Moses?

☐ with a title only

☐ through Moses' family

God always gets to choose how he discloses himself to people, Moses included. But in this moment, as the tree burns in front of him, the most important thing Moses needs to hear is that this God is the one, true, living God whom his ancestors followed. Just as many of us trust others faster when a family member or trusted friend recommends the relationship, this connection to Moses' forefathers is a signal that God can be trusted.

5. Review Exodus 3:6 and note Moses' response to God's self-revelation. What does Moses do?

Moses responds exactly how I would have—in fear. This ridiculous (and yet so relatable) reaction reminds me of Adam and Eve's attempt to hide from God in the Garden of Eden. Intuitively we know that being in God's presence is a holy encounter, worthy of our reverence. But sometimes that reverence comes out sideways as fear and an impulse to hide from the God who sees us.

In this theophany or appearance of the Divine, the Divine is identified as the god of Abraham, Isaac, and Jacob (3:6). Linking the God of the exodus with the God of Genesis identifies the God of patriarchal promises with the God who delivers the Israelites.[7]

Nyasha Junior, "Exodus," in *Women's Bible Commentary*

---

6. In Exodus 3:10, God tells Moses that Moses will be God's instrument to deliver the Israelites from Egyptian slavery. Write out what Moses says in response in Exodus 3:11.

Who am I? Before we judge Moses for his response, think about the identity baggage he was carrying. Born to Hebrew slaves, cast out of the Egyptian palace, exiled into Midian after committing murder. He'd gone from being connected to royalty to joining his new father-in-law as a shepherd. I'd guess he spent many pensive hours watching the sheep, reliving the change in location and vocation that had brought him so far from the only life he'd ever known. Hearing God call him back must have sparked a deep identity crisis. Him? Back to Egypt? To free the Hebrew slaves?

Thanks to author Ruth Haley Barton, I suspect Moses was also dealing with imposter syndrome, wondering how he could possibly be the right person to lead God's people out of Egypt.[8] When God told Moses he'd heard the Jewish cries for help, Moses started asking questions that anyone might ask: *Who am I that I should go? How is this going to work out? What am I supposed to tell people to get them to believe me?*

The Burning Bush was the inauguration of a God-sized mission to free the Jews from slavery. As Moses faced an inconsumable God in that Burning Bush, he also stared at a sacred responsibility—and many leadership crucibles ahead. Nothing about himself or his journey gave him confidence that he could pull it off. As Carmen Joy Imes put it in her book *Bearing God's Name: Why Sinai Still Matters*, "Moses was God's designated special agent for this rescue operation. But Moses was not buying it."[9]

How did Moses push past imposter syndrome to step obediently into God's commissioning? Moses focused on God's identity, not his own. The God who spoke from the Burning Bush was the same God of Abraham, Isaac, Jacob, and

> The fire in the bush is self-sustaining. It needs no fuel. It blazes as it chooses. Similarly, God is self-subsistent and self-determining. He will be who he chooses to be.[10]
>
> Richard Bauckham, *Who Is God?*

Joseph. The same covenant-keeping God who promised to bless his people so that they could be a blessing to all.

If we are paralyzed in the face of God's current assignment for our own lives, we may need to refocus our attention. *It's not about how unqualified we may feel—but about the God we follow.* If we focus on him instead of on our ability, our pasts, and the difficulties ahead, God's powerful presence in our lives will give us the courage to face our fears and go anyway.

7. **If you are struggling with an identity crisis or imposter syndrome, describe how those struggles show up in your life.**

8. **What truths about God's identity can reorient your focus away from how you feel and toward his calling on your life?**

PART 3

UNDERSTANDING

Now that we've finished a close reading of the Scriptures, we're going to spend some time on interpretation: doing our best to understand what God was saying to the original audience and what he's teaching us through the process. But to do so, we need to learn his ways and consider how God's Word would have been understood by the original audience before applying the same truths to our own lives. "Scripture interpretation" may sound a little stuffy, but understanding what God means to communicate to us in the Bible is crucial to enjoying a close relationship with Jesus. Part 3 will enable you to answer the question *What does it mean?*

AMID THE FLAMES of the Burning Bush scene, several truths about God and his work in our lives become clear:

- God keeps his promises.
- God hears the cries of the oppressed and is our great Rescuer.
- Moses is like a new Adam, Abraham, Isaac, Jacob, and Joseph, leading God's people toward redemption.
- As we pay attention to the out-of-the-ordinary events in our lives, God may invite us to deeper faith.

These truths are meaningful, and we could spend pages interpreting them. But as we take a closer look at this tree, I want to suggest that the main point of the Burning Bush story is to show God's people, by way of Moses, who God is.

One of my favorite Bible scholars, L. Michael Morales, beautifully summarizes the purpose of God's self-revelation:

> Clearly, Israel has not retained a knowledge of the "God of your fathers." . . . The first half of Exodus restores a knowledge of Yahweh to the world through the exodus.[11]

God's people had forgotten who he was. What did they need most? A reminder that he is "I AM." And how does God first choose to reveal that he is the God who can be trusted to rescue? A conversation at a tree on fire and yet not consumed.

1. **Reread Exodus 3:1–18. List everything you learn about God's character from the Burning Bush encounter.**

2. **How would these revelations and reminders of who God is impact Moses' life?**

3. How does God say the Israelites will respond to Moses when he tells them I AM sent him to lead them out of Egypt (Exodus 3:18)?

When God declared that the Israelites would listen to Moses, he was proclaiming that the people would listen to God himself. Moses was God's representative, his vice-regent for the Exodus rescue operation.

God's people were ignorant about God's identity, but God promised that once they knew who he was and what Moses had been sent to do, they would listen. This must have been incredibly reassuring to Moses as he struggled with identity crisis and imposter syndrome. Whenever his confidence waned, he could remember that the faithful God of his fathers, not Moses' own ability, guaranteed the outcome.

MAKING CONNECTIONS

An important part of understanding the meaning of a Bible passage is getting a sense of its place in the broader storyline of Scripture. When we make connections between different parts of the Bible, we get a glimpse of the unity and cohesion of the Scriptures.

So far, we've explored the trees in the Garden of Eden and the burning tree on Mount Sinai. The two stories are connected, and not just because they are both in the Bible or in the Old Testament. Because God's story of redemption is one cohesive unit pointing to God revealing himself in Christ, we discover that tree imagery in the Bible represents far more than just a piece of wood with branches and fruit. Trees carry great significance in the storyline of Scripture.

In both the stories we've read so far, trees are places of decisions. We see that often when the people of God happen upon a tree, they have a conversation with God or about God that requires them to make a choice.

The same choice lies before us. Will we listen to God? Will we take notice when he is trying to get our attention? Will we trust who he is and his calling on our lives? Or will we ignore his voice, focus on our own ability, and take matters in our own hands?

Moses listened to the voice of God again and again through the dramatic exodus from Egypt and the long journey through the wilderness. But at a pivotal point in Moses' leadership, God speaks—and Moses chooses to go his own way.

4. Read Numbers 20:1–12 and underline every mention of a stick or staff.

20 In the first month the whole Israelite community arrived at the Desert of Zin, and they stayed at Kadesh. There Miriam died and was buried.

² Now there was no water for the community, and the people gathered in opposition to Moses and Aaron. ³ They quarreled with Moses and said, "If only we had died when our brothers fell dead before the LORD! ⁴ Why did you bring the LORD's community into this wilderness, that we and our livestock should die here? ⁵ Why did you bring us up out of Egypt to this terrible place? It has no grain or figs, grapevines or pomegranates. And there is no water to drink!"

⁶ Moses and Aaron went from the assembly to the entrance to the tent of meeting and fell facedown, and the glory of the LORD appeared to them. ⁷ The LORD said to Moses, ⁸ "Take the staff, and you and your brother Aaron gather the assembly together. Speak to that rock before their eyes and it will pour out its water. You will bring water out of the rock for the community so they and their livestock can drink."

⁹ So Moses took the staff from the LORD's presence, just as he commanded him. ¹⁰ He and Aaron gathered the assembly together in front of the rock and Moses said to them, "Listen, you rebels, must we bring you water out of this rock?" ¹¹ Then Moses raised his arm and struck the rock twice with his staff. Water gushed out, and the community and their livestock drank.

¹² But the LORD said to Moses and Aaron, "Because you did not trust in

me enough to honor me as holy in the sight of the Israelites, you will not bring this community into the land I give them."

NUMBERS 20:1-12, NIV

5. What did God tell Moses to do? What did Moses do instead?

6. How do Moses' words and actions demonstrate self-reliance rather than God-dependence?

7. What is the biggest decision you need to make right now? What voices are you listening to?

I wonder if somewhere along the journey, Moses began to subconsciously see himself, not God, as the Israelites' leader. There's a striking difference between what happens in Numbers 20 and what we see in an earlier, similar situation. In Exodus 17, Moses is undone by the Israelites' behavior and begs God not just for water but for rescue:

"What am I to do with these people? They are almost ready to stone me."
EXODUS 17:4, NIV

But this time, years later, Moses does not ask anything of God. We do not see a request for help or signs of dependence, just expectation that God will do what he did before. And it seems as though Moses' rage at the Israelites' complaining drowns out God's instructions. Moses reacts out of anger, with biting words and aggressive action—when God had simply told him to speak to the rock.

And because Moses chose to listen to his own anger above God's voice, because he didn't pay attention to what God was up to with the command to speak rather than to strike—his lack of trust kept him from the Promised Land.

Being curious about what God is up to and paying attention to his voice and his words is the path to life. God wants to meet our needs and lead us into freedom. Will we pay attention so we can follow?

— — —

Let's check back in on our Sticks Storyline.

THE STICKS STORYLINE OF SCRIPTURE

Stick(s)	Element of Fire	The Decision
the Tree of Life & the Tree of the Knowledge of Good and Evil (Genesis 2–3)	Flaming swords of the cherubim guard the Garden of Eden after the exile.	Will we choose to live wisely with wisdom from God or try to take matters into our own hands?
the Burning Bush (Exodus 3)	The Sinai tree/bush is in flames but is not consumed.	Will we take notice when God is trying get our attention or ignore his voice and keep moving on?
the Messiah Tree (Isaiah 1, 6, 11, 53)	The smoke in the Temple and the flaming coals burn with heat from the fire.	Will we branch out from our shady family trees and grow deep roots in God's family?
the True Vine, Jesus (John 15)	The branches who do not abide in Jesus wither and are used as firewood.	Will we stay connected to Jesus for a fruitful life or try to produce good fruit on our own?
the Tree of Life (Revelation 22)	If you choose to live outside the Garden City gates, you will be cast into a lake of fire.	Will we choose to reframe our perspective or follow old patterns?

Fear Response	Consequences of the Wrong Choice	Wise Choice
Adam and Eve hide from God between the trees out of fear and shame.	When Adam and Eve choose to seek wisdom for themselves, they end up exiled from Eden.	Trust God to give us wisdom through an ongoing relationship with him.
Moses hides his face from God at the Burning Bush out of fear.	If the Israelites don't choose to follow Moses in the Exodus, they will remain in Egypt as slaves and exiles.	Notice, listen to, and trust God's voice when he's trying to get our attention.
The prophet Isaiah asks God how long his judgment will last, fearing none will survive.	Since the Israelites choose idolatry, God allows them to be exiled from Jerusalem and enslaved to the Babylonians and Assyrians.	Remain faithful to God, knowing he's always going to be faithful to us.
Jesus quickly encourages his followers that his friendship and love for them does not waver, as if he knows his words will cause fear.	Those who do not choose to abide in Christ will be exiled to fire, where all efforts will be consumed and reduced to ashes.	Stay close to Jesus to bear good fruit.
There will be no more fear in the new heaven and new earth.	If we do not choose to follow Christ, the Tree of Life, we will be exiled to the lake of fire.	Choose to live near the Tree of Life.

1. What choice are you facing right now? How can you pay attention to where God is at work?

2. What did you learn about God's character in this lesson?

3. How should these truths shape your faith community and change you?

RESPONDING

The purpose of Bible study is to help you become more Christlike; that's why part 4 will include journaling space for your reflection on and responses to the content and a blank checklist for actionable next steps. You'll be able to process what you're learning so that you can live out the concepts and pursue Christlikeness. Part 4 will enable you to answer the questions *What truths is this passage teaching?* and *How do I apply this to my life?*

TO NOTICE WHEN GOD is trying to get our attention and listen to the voice of God, we first need to watch for where God is working—and that can be a challenge. It took an inconsumable tree on fire to grab Moses' attention. Our lives today are full of so much noise—the echoes of our past, the distractions of our present, the whispers of what's up ahead—that it can be difficult to remember to watch for the ways God is showing up.

Personally, I find it very difficult to look up from whatever project has my laser-beam focus. I tend to put my head down at work or in ministry and "crank." I rush through my days with the hope that I'll get through my priorities, and at the end of it all I have margin for almost nothing else besides my family. Sometimes even my family has to call my name several times in a row, growing in volume with each address, to shake me from my phone or divert my attention from my inboxes. I know I'm not alone in this struggle. You may know a thing or two about being uninterruptible, singularly focused, or in the weeds.

But this kind of pace causes us to miss the flames in front of us. Spiritual director and author Ruth Haley Barton points us to the importance of paying attention:

> All of us have burning bushes in our lives, places that shimmer with grace, alerting us to the possibility that God is at work doing something that we could not have predicted. . . .
>
> If spiritual leadership is anything, it is the capacity to see the bush burning in the middle of our own life and having enough sense to turn aside, take off our shoes and pay attention![12]

As painful as it is to admit, I don't often have enough sense to pause and reflect on God's activity in my life. But when I do, it's because I'm asking questions: *Where is God making himself known in my life? Where is his activity completely obvious but in surprising ways?*

As we keep our eyes on the tree line of Scripture, let's remember to be watchful for where God is showing up in our lives—and to trust him when he speaks. When burning bushes show up, we can respond to God in three ways.

1. PAUSE AND REFLECT WHEN SOMETHING IS OUT OF THE ORDINARY.

Let something catch you off guard. When you notice your surroundings have changed, the atmosphere has shifted, or your loved one's responses sound different, take a moment to pause and be curious. Don't breeze past something that is out of the ordinary. Instead, pause long enough for a couple of deep breaths, then reflect long enough to put a note in your phone, detailing the things that seem out of sync.

In my own life, these brief moments of contemplation are opportunities to talk with God about his desire for my freedom in Christ. Much like at the Burning Bush, God is working right now to help us find freedom. But let's not miss how he might be alerting us to his activity. Pause and reflect when something is out of the ordinary. You never know—you could be stumbling upon holy ground with your Savior.

2. LISTEN TO GOD'S VOICE INSTEAD OF YOUR INNER CRITIC.

The loop in your head, that broken record of negative self-talk, not only will bring you down—it can drown out God's voice too. I'm so grateful Moses listened to God's voice of commissioning and comfort. He must have wrestled to internalize the radical declaration from God that Moses would lead the people out of Egypt. I wonder if the mental tape in his head started to play: *You're a murderer, a coward. You're only a shepherd. Your people don't respect you; you're a deserter.* I know that's how I would have responded to God's voice at the Burning Bush. But you and I have a choice to make: We can listen to God and trust him, or we can listen to ourselves and our inner critic. In the same way the Burning Bush was a decision tree for Moses, our own burning bushes are decision trees too. Choose to trust God's voice, every time.

3. ASK GOD YOUR BURNING QUESTIONS. HE CAN HANDLE THEM.

Moses was brave enough and stayed long enough in God's presence to pepper him with some burning questions. Why him? How would people respond? What should he say when they asked who God is? I wonder if at this point Moses' eyes were watering from the bright glow of the tree in flames. Was he sweating through his clothes because of the heat from the fire? Did he feel tempted to step away? Whatever the case, Moses persevered with his questions—and God didn't reprimand him for doing so. God didn't shame Moses for his fear or lack of courage. He didn't curse him or tell him to keep quiet. God allowed for Moses' questions, and he does the same for yours and mine. God can handle your fears and doubts. Your burning questions are welcome. Ask away.

Use this journaling space to process what you are learning.

Ask yourself how these truths impact your relationship with God and with others.

What is the Holy Spirit bringing to your mind as actionable next steps in your faith journey?

-

-

-

BRANCHING OUT FROM YOUR SHADY FAMILY TREE

THE MESSIAH TREE:
WHERE GOD'S PEOPLE FIND HOPE FOR THE FUTURE

SCRIPTURE: ISAIAH 1, 6, 11, 53

CONTEXT

Before you begin your study, we will start with the context of the story we are about to read together: the setting, both cultural and historical; the people involved; and where our passage fits in the larger setting of Scripture. All these things help us make sense of what we're reading. Understanding the context of a Bible story is fundamental to reading Scripture well. Getting your bearings before you read will enable you to answer the question *What am I about to read?*

I THINK OAK TREES ARE BEAUTIFUL, but they can also be a bit overwhelming. Tall oak trees surrounded an apartment my husband and I used to live in, and the acorns drove me nuts. They littered the walkways in every direction, and sometimes they'd pelt me or my windshield as they dropped to the ground.

Those oak trees came to mind as I tried to focus in on only five trees for this study. Every time I'd clear a path, I'd find more trees spread throughout the Bible and get distracted.

- *Tree imagery in Noah's story*: an ark of wood (Genesis 6), an olive branch signaling the end of the Flood (Genesis 8)

- *Tree imagery in Abraham's story*: the Lord appearing to him by the oaks or terebinths of Mamre (Genesis 18); the ram caught in the tree branches as a substitution for Isaac (Genesis 22)

- *Tree imagery throughout the rest of the book of Exodus*: Moses using his wooden staff to demonstrate God's power to Pharaoh (Exodus 7); Moses striking a rock with that same staff to provide water for the people (Exodus 17)

- *Tree imagery in Judges*: Deborah judging from under a tree (Judges 4); Gideon being called into judgeship from under a tree (Judges 6)

- *Tree imagery throughout prophetic literature*: the prophet Amos taking care of sycamore trees (Amos 7); the prophet Jonah pouting under a tree God had caused to grow (Jonah 4); the prophet Jeremiah describing people as trees that need to be planted near water (Jeremiah 17)

And then, as I was writing, *BibleProject*—my favorite podcast—launched a whole series on trees in the Bible.[1] As if I didn't already have enough trees to survey!

But as I continued to clear all these pathways, I found myself returning to one tree that felt particularly important in the storyline of Scripture: the Messiah Tree in Isaiah.

Nestled in the branches of our faith-family tree is a whole lot of poor decision making. What we see through all the patriarchs in the Old Testament, and all the kings, and all the judges, through all the covenants, is that God's people need a Savior. The patriarchs proved to be insufficient, making many decisions that were questionable at best and sinful at worst. The kings proved to be insufficient rulers, never fully obedient to God or his ways. The judges proved to be insufficient at judging the nation of Israel, often behaving in shady ways. And the people of God never fulfilled their side of any of the covenants with God. Just like us, they tried their best (or didn't) and came up short.

> If the Old Testament had a tree nursery in it, it would be found in the book of Isaiah.[2]
>
> Matthew Sleeth, *Reforesting Faith*

A survey of the Old Testament shows us that God's people need more—someone able to branch out from such a shady family history and save us.

The prophet Isaiah ushered in the possibility that a messiah, or savior, was coming. Even Isaiah's name meant "Yahweh is salvation." Isaiah prophesied during the reigns of four kings—Uzziah, Jotham, Ahaz, and Hezekiah—writing to a group of weary Israelites who had chosen to be unfaithful to God. Isaiah had a tough job: He was instructed by God to announce the destruction and exile of God's people because of their unfaithfulness. His audience was suffering the consequences of their sin—exile from their home, Jerusalem. In the book of Isaiah, both the Assyrians and Babylonians rise to power and punish God's people. The Israelites were facing a watershed moment, a crisis of their faith. Could God rescue them from their sin? Would they choose to repent?

God didn't leave his people in despair. The book of Isaiah is also about the possibility of a new reality—a world where a small root of hope, Jesus, shoots out of an old stump, Israel.

Together, we are going to see just how far God's people can branch out from their faith history—and in turn, how we can branch out from our own shady family trees.

1. **PERSONAL CONTEXT: What is going on in your life right now that might impact how you understand these Bible passages?**

2. **SPIRITUAL CONTEXT: If you've never studied these passages before, what piques your curiosity? If you've studied these passages before, what impressions and insights do you recall? What problems or concerns might you have with the passages?**

PART 2

SEEING

Seeing the text is vital if we want the heart of the Scripture passage to sink in. We read slowly and intentionally through the text with the context in mind. As we practice close, thoughtful reading of Scripture, we pick up on phrases, implications, and meanings we might otherwise have missed. Part 2 includes close Scripture reading and observation questions to empower you to answer the question *What is the story saying?*

THE BOOK OF ISAIAH starts with a startling and convicting sermon about the Israelites' refusal to obey God. God is exasperated with his people, and Isaiah is here to tell them the truth.

1. **Read Isaiah 1:7-17 and underline any mention of trees, vineyards, or branches.**

> ⁷ Your country lies desolate,
>> your cities are burned with fire;
>
> in your very presence
>> aliens devour your land;
>>
>> it is desolate, as overthrown by foreigners.
>
> ⁸ And daughter Zion is left
>> like a booth in a vineyard,

like a shelter in a cucumber field,
    like a besieged city.
9 If the LORD of hosts
    had not left us a few survivors,
we would have been like Sodom,
    and become like Gomorrah.

10 Hear the word of the LORD,
    you rulers of Sodom!
Listen to the teaching of our God,
    you people of Gomorrah!
11 What to me is the multitude of your sacrifices?
    says the LORD;
I have had enough of burnt offerings of rams
    and the fat of fed beasts;
I do not delight in the blood of bulls,
    or of lambs, or of goats.

12 When you come to appear before me,
    who asked this from your hand?
    Trample my courts no more;
13 bringing offerings is futile;
    incense is an abomination to me.
New moon and sabbath and calling of convocation—
    I cannot endure solemn assemblies with iniquity.
14 Your new moons and your appointed festivals
    my soul hates;
they have become a burden to me,
    I am weary of bearing them.
15 When you stretch out your hands,
    I will hide my eyes from you;
even though you make many prayers,

I will not listen;

    your hands are full of blood.

¹⁶ Wash yourselves; make yourselves clean;

    remove the evil of your doings

    from before my eyes;

cease to do evil,

    ¹⁷ learn to do good;

seek justice,

    rescue the oppressed,

defend the orphan,

    plead for the widow.

ISAIAH 1:7-17

2. In one or two sentences, describe the state of Israel.

3. How does God feel about Israel's rebellion? Check all that apply.

☐ God believes Israel is as bad as Sodom and Gomorrah, cities that burned to the ground for the sin of their people.

☐ God is tired of Israel's sacrifices because their hearts are not turned toward him.

☐ God is weary of Israel's religious activity because the people are just going through the motions.

☐ God wishes Israel would cease doing evil and learn to do good and seek justice.

Isaiah's prophecy continues with a preview of Israel's future if they repent of their sin—or, conversely, if they dig in their heels.

4. **Read Isaiah 1:27-31 and underline any mention of trees, vineyards, or branches.**

    27 Zion shall be redeemed by justice,
       and those in her who repent, by righteousness.
    28 But rebels and sinners shall be destroyed together,
       and those who forsake the LORD shall be consumed.
    29 For you shall be ashamed of the oaks
       in which you delighted;
    and you shall blush for the gardens
       that you have chosen.
    30 For you shall be like an oak
       whose leaf withers,
       and like a garden without water.
    31 The strong shall become like tinder,
       and their work like a spark;
    they and their work shall burn together,
       with no one to quench them.

    ISAIAH 1:27-31

5. **Using Isaiah 1:27 as your guide, write out the hopeful future Israel has for those who repent of their rebellion.**

6. **What is the image God gives Isaiah in Isaiah 1:30-31? What will Israel become if they don't repent?**

Imagine the Israelites hearing Isaiah's sermon for the first time, listening to the stern warning that without repentance, Israel was destined to be firewood and eventually just ashes. I wonder if their memories jumped back to the Garden of Eden—God's primordial vision of the world as a flourishing garden where people chose to live wisely and obediently. Would the Israelites connect Isaiah's image of burnt firewood to the fire of the cherubim guarding the Garden of Eden?

My heart aches for Israel because I can relate to their wayward inclinations. I long to please God and live in a way that honors him and helps others—but I'm only human. I often reject obedience for my own gratification.

What Isaiah preaches to the exiled people of God is still relevant for you and me today because his point is that our sins have consequences. God will be patient with us the way he was patient with the Israelites. But we will be held accountable. The only way out for the Israelites, and for us, is to repent of our sins and turn back to God.

7. **Repentance requires humility, honesty, and self-awareness. Sit quietly with the Lord for a moment. If the Holy Spirit brings to mind something you need to repent of, write it down here.**

Isaiah's book starts with a jolting message from God but little information about who Isaiah is and how he came into his role as a herald of God's judgment. We don't learn more about Isaiah's call into ministry until Isaiah 6. As Isaiah describes his vision of God in his Temple and his encounter with God himself, notice the unifying patterns of Isaiah's setting. Literary threads connect this throne-room scene to the trees in the Garden of Eden and to the Burning Bush.

8. Read Isaiah 6:1-13 and underline anything related to trees and fire.

6 In the year that King Uzziah died, I saw the Lord sitting on a throne, high and lofty; and the hem of his robe filled the temple. ² Seraphs were in attendance above him; each had six wings: with two they covered their faces, and with two they covered their feet, and with two they flew. ³ And one called to another and said:

"Holy, holy, holy is the LORD of hosts;
the whole earth is full of his glory."

⁴ The pivots on the thresholds shook at the voices of those who called, and the house filled with smoke. ⁵ And I said: "Woe is me! I am lost, for I am a man of unclean lips, and I live among a people of unclean lips; yet my eyes have seen the King, the LORD of hosts!"

⁶ Then one of the seraphs flew to me, holding a live coal that had been taken from the altar with a pair of tongs. ⁷ The seraph touched my mouth with it and said: "Now that this has touched your lips, your guilt has departed and your sin is blotted out." ⁸ Then I heard the voice of the Lord saying, "Whom shall I send, and who will go for us?" And I said, "Here am I; send me!" ⁹ And he said, "Go and say to this people:

'Keep listening, but do not comprehend;
keep looking, but do not understand.'
¹⁰ Make the mind of this people dull,
 and stop their ears,
 and shut their eyes,
so that they may not look with their eyes,
 and listen with their ears,
and comprehend with their minds,
 and turn and be healed."
¹¹ Then I said, "How long, O Lord?" And he said:
"Until cities lie waste

without inhabitant,
and houses without people,
and the land is utterly desolate;
^{12} until the LORD sends everyone far away,
and vast is the emptiness in the midst of the land.
^{13} Even if a tenth part remain in it,
it will be burned again,
like a terebinth or an oak
whose stump remains standing
when it is felled."
The holy seed is its stump.

ISAIAH 6:1-13

9. What do you imagine Isaiah would have been thinking during this encounter with God?

The hope in this section is in the very last sentence of Isaiah 6:13: "The holy seed is its stump." Even after judgment that will be like a fire consuming a city, a stump will survive, and a holy seed inside it will sprout to life.

Notice with me the connection between Isaiah's moment of calling to the prophetic ministry and the way the Messiah is talked about as a stump.

10. Read Isaiah 11:1-3 and underline what makes the Messiah different from the Israelites.

11 A shoot shall come out from the stump of Jesse,
and a branch shall grow out of his roots.

² The spirit of the LORD shall rest on him,

    the spirit of wisdom and understanding,

    the spirit of counsel and might,

    the spirit of knowledge and the fear of the LORD.

³ His delight shall be in the fear of the LORD.

ISAIAH 11:1-3

Isaiah says that a Messiah is coming to Israel who will be wholly devoted to God, unlike the rebellious Israelites. The Savior will have the spirit of the Lord resting on him so that he is full of wisdom, understanding, counsel, might, knowledge, and the fear of the Lord. Basically, this shoot from the stump of Jesse will be everything the people of God are currently not. Whatever they lack, the Messiah will fulfill.

PART 3

UNDERSTANDING

Now that we've finished a close reading of the Scriptures, we're going to spend some time on interpretation: doing our best to understand what God was saying to the original audience and what he's teaching us through the process. But to do so, we need to learn his ways and consider how God's Word would have been understood by the original audience before applying the same truths to our own lives. "Scripture interpretation" may sound a little stuffy, but understanding what God means to communicate to us in the Bible is crucial to enjoying a close relationship with Jesus. Part 3 will enable you to answer the question *What does it mean?*

ISAIAH'S PROPHECIES ARE CLEAR: God was going to purify the people of God through the furnace of judgment. And when the purifying process was over, the remnant that remained would be a suffering servant. The promise of the suffering servant, the shoot of Jesse, the branch coming out of the stump of Israel, would one day be fulfilled in Jesus. Jesus the Messiah is the ultimate fulfillment of Isaiah's prophecies.

1. **Read Isaiah 53:2-6 and put a check next to anything that is true of both the suffering servant Isaiah describes and Jesus.**

   ² **For he grew up before him like a young plant,**
   and like a root out of dry ground;

The remnant is that group of people who survive some catastrophe brought about by God, ordinarily in judgment for sin. This group become the nucleus for the continuation of humankind or the people of God. This surviving remnant inherits the promises of God afresh; the future existence of a larger group will grow from this purified, holy remnant that has undergone and survived divine judgment.[4]

Tremper Longman III and Raymond B. Dillard, *An Introduction to the Old Testament*

he had no form or majesty that we should look at him,
    nothing in his appearance that we should desire him.
3 He was despised and rejected by others;
    a man of suffering and acquainted with infirmity;
and as one from whom others hide their faces
    he was despised, and we held him of no account.

4 Surely he has borne our infirmities
    and carried our diseases;
yet we accounted him stricken,
    struck down by God, and afflicted.
5 But he was wounded for our transgressions,
    crushed for our iniquities;
upon him was the punishment that made us whole,
    and by his bruises we are healed.
6 All we like sheep have gone astray;
    we have all turned to our own way,
and the Lord has laid on him
    the iniquity of us all.

ISAIAH 53:2-6

Had I been the author of the redemption story, my hero would have come on the scene as a dominant, conquering warrior. Instead, the Messiah God sends comes to us humble and lowly.

2. **List at least three ways the suffering servant is different from our normal expectations of the hero of a story.**

3. **According to Isaiah 53:5, what would the suffering servant accomplish for Israel?**

MAKING CONNECTIONS

An important part of understanding the meaning of a Bible passage is getting a sense of its place in the broader storyline of Scripture. When we make connections between different parts of the Bible, we get a glimpse of the unity and cohesion of the Scriptures.

The prophets in the Old Testament were speaking to particular people in a particular time, and yet we see throughout the Gospels that God was working through the prophets to point toward the ultimate fulfillment of their words: when God himself would step into the world he made to redeem and restore those broken down by sin.

Jesus himself showed the people the deliberate connection between the words of the prophet Isaiah and Jesus' incarnated life and ministry:

¹⁶ He went to Nazareth, where he had been brought up, and on the Sabbath day he went into the synagogue, as was his custom. He stood up to read, ¹⁷ and the scroll of the prophet Isaiah was handed to him. Unrolling it, he found the place where it is written:

¹⁸ "The Spirit of the Lord is on me,
> because he has anointed me
> to proclaim good news to the poor.
He has sent me to proclaim freedom for the prisoners
> and recovery of sight for the blind,
to set the oppressed free,
> ¹⁹ to proclaim the year of the Lord's favor."

²⁰ Then he rolled up the scroll, gave it back to the attendant and sat down. The eyes of everyone in the synagogue were fastened on him. ²¹ He began by saying to them, "Today this scripture is fulfilled in your hearing."

LUKE 4:16-21, NIV

Similarly, we find the suffering-servant passage fulfilled throughout the life of Jesus.

4. **Match the description of the suffering servant with the passage from the New Testament that describes its ultimate fulfillment.**

JESUS IS THE SUFFERING SERVANT

He was despised and rejected by others	1 Peter 2:24
Surely he has borne our infirmities and carried our diseases	Galatians 3:13
Yet we accounted him stricken, struck down by God, and afflicted	Hebrews 10:14
But he was wounded for our transgressions, crushed for our iniquities	John 1:10–11
Upon him was the punishment that made us whole	Matthew 8:17
And by his bruises we are healed	Romans 4:25

Isaiah spoke his words to a hurting people experiencing the consequences of unfaithfulness. As the life, death, and resurrection of Jesus show us, though, exile is never the end of God's story. We are never abandoned.

5. Where do you feel stuck in exile?

6. How does the ultimate faithfulness of God encourage you to remain faithful yourself?

The Messiah Tree the prophet Isaiah alludes to throughout his book finds its ultimate fulfillment in Jesus. Jesus is the remnant of one. Jesus is the embodiment of Israel living in perfect obedience to God. In the same way that Israel faced divine judgment as a nation, Jesus suffered on the cross. In the same way that Israel as a nation experienced exile, Jesus willingly chose to be forsaken by God—and in the grave, exiled from God—for three days. In the same way that Israel as a nation was restored time and time again to God, Jesus was restored and resurrected from the dead. In the same way that Israel always had a remnant that survived God's judgment, Jesus gave birth to the New Testament church, a remnant of God's faithful people who would inherit God's promises to his

He has not *required* human sacrifice; he has himself *become* the human sacrifice. He has not turned *us* over and forsaken *us*; he was *himself* turned over and forsaken.[5]

Fleming Rutledge, *And God Spoke to Abraham*

people. Jesus is the suffering servant who came to redeem Israel—and the Savior of the whole world.

— — —

Let's check back in on our Sticks Storyline.

THE STICKS STORYLINE OF SCRIPTURE

Stick(s)	Element of Fire	The Decision
the Tree of Life & the Tree of the Knowledge of Good and Evil (Genesis 2–3)	Flaming swords of the cherubim guard the Garden of Eden after the exile.	Will we choose to live wisely with wisdom from God or try to take matters into our own hands?
the Burning Bush (Exodus 3)	The Sinai tree/bush is in flames but is not consumed.	Will we take notice when God is trying get our attention or ignore his voice and keep moving on?
the Messiah Tree (Isaiah 1, 6, 11, 53)	The smoke in the Temple and the flaming coals burn with heat from the fire.	Will we branch out from our shady family trees and grow deep roots in God's family?
the True Vine, Jesus (John 15)	The branches who do not abide in Jesus wither and are used as firewood.	Will we stay connected to Jesus for a fruitful life or try to produce good fruit on our own?
the Tree of Life (Revelation 22)	If you choose to live outside the Garden City gates, you will be cast into a lake of fire.	Will we choose to reframe our perspective or follow old patterns?

Fear Response	Consequences of the Wrong Choice	Wise Choice
Adam and Eve hide from God between the trees out of fear and shame.	When Adam and Eve choose to seek wisdom for themselves, they end up exiled from Eden.	Trust God to give us wisdom through an ongoing relationship with him.
Moses hides his face from God at the Burning Bush out of fear.	If the Israelites don't choose to follow Moses in the Exodus, they will remain in Egypt as slaves and exiles.	Notice, listen to, and trust God's voice when he's trying to get our attention.
The prophet Isaiah asks God how long his judgment will last, fearing none will survive.	Since the Israelites choose idolatry, God allows them to be exiled from Jerusalem and enslaved to the Babylonians and Assyrians.	Remain faithful to God, knowing he's always going to be faithful to us.
Jesus quickly encourages his followers that his friendship and love for them does not waver, as if he knows his words will cause fear.	Those who do not choose to abide in Christ will be exiled to fire, where all efforts will be consumed and reduced to ashes.	Stay close to Jesus to bear good fruit.
There will be no more fear in the new heaven and new earth.	If we do not choose to follow Christ, the Tree of Life, we will be exiled to the lake of fire.	Choose to live near the Tree of Life.

1. **What choice are you facing right now? How can you pay attention to where God is at work?**

2. **What did you learn about God's character in this lesson?**

3. **How should these truths shape your faith community and change you?**

RESPONDING

The purpose of Bible study is to help you become more Christlike; that's why part 4 will include journaling space for your reflection on and responses to the content and a blank checklist for actionable next steps. You'll be able to process what you're learning so that you can live out the concepts and pursue Christlikeness. Part 4 will enable you to answer the questions *What truths is this passage teaching?* and *How do I apply this to my life?*

ISAIAH HAD A HARD JOB—to preach about the impending judgment coming on the Israelites at the hands of political superpowers like the Babylonians and Assyrians. The people must have felt helpless and powerless.

God's people had spent a long time making the wrong choices—ones that moved them further away from him. Adam and Eve didn't get it right, and they were exiled from the Garden of Eden. Noah's contemporaries didn't get it right, and they were exiled to death through the Flood. The patriarchs—men who heard from God, like Abraham, Isaac, Jacob, and Joseph—didn't get it right, and they didn't get to see all God's promises fulfilled. Moses didn't get it all right, and even he missed out on the Promised Land. The judges didn't get it right, which is why God gave the people kings. And when the kings didn't get it right, God's people needed a Messiah.

If this feels weighty to you, you're understanding the biblical concept of sin correctly. Everyone falls short of God's glory. And there are serious consequences for choosing to be unfaithful to God. You and I share a faith history with all the people who worshiped God in the Old Testament. And we have to be honest about that history: Our family tree is pretty shady. We are a motley crew of screwups and sinners.

But be encouraged: We are not doomed to our shady family tree's mess-ups. Even if we are burned down to a stump, Jesus sprouts out as our seed of hope. And we see glimmers of hope in the faithful few throughout history. There have always been godly people living wisely and honoring God with their lives.

On a personal level, the trees in Isaiah's book bring me great hope for my own family tree. For generations, one side of my family has suffered under the combination of untreated mental illness and substance abuse. If generational curses are a thing, we have one. And its effects have had a devastating, catastrophic impact on my loved ones.

If the weight of our faith ancestors has you smoldering with anxiety, or your own family tree has you worried your future will end up in ashes, hear me on this: You are not doomed by your family tree. Branching out is Jesus' specialty.

1. YOU ARE NOT DOOMED BY YOUR SHADY FAMILY TREE.

At one point in high school, after learning how many branches in my family tree were broken through tragic deaths, I started to feel doomed. Breaking free from the generational curses rooted in my family tree felt impossible. I was terrified until I began going through a Bible study by Beth Moore called *Breaking Free*. In one of the lessons, Beth asked the reader to draw out their family tree and imagine Jesus replanting us to grow a new branch. It changed the course of my life, and by God's grace, Caleb is now the beneficiary of our newly sprouting family unit. We are growing up in the way of Jesus together.

2. BRANCHING OUT IS JESUS' SPECIALTY. GO AHEAD AND BLOOM WHERE YOU ARE PLANTED.

If thousands of years of faith history have proven anything, it is that Jesus has power over darkness in our world and in our own hearts. If Jesus branched out of a wicked and perverse generation that was unwilling to repent, you can branch out and bear good fruit too. As speaker and author Jill Briscoe would say, bloom where you are planted.[6] It may feel like you're planted in something like a stump, but Jesus has shown us what he can grow from such humble roots.

When we follow the Messiah, our roots are not in our families' past sins or Satan's victories. We are planted next to our water source, Jesus. And his wisdom will help us flourish in all the seasons of life, as good or hard as they may be. You may still share some of your ancestors' struggles, but you are not fated to them.

J-E-S-U-S has replanted me. He can do the same for you. Yes, he can.

Use this journaling space to process what you are learning.

Ask yourself how these truths impact your relationship with God and with others.

What is the Holy Spirit bringing to your mind as actionable next steps in your faith journey?

-

-

-

STAYING CONNECTED TO JESUS FOR A FRUITFUL LIFE

**THE TRUE VINE, JESUS:
WHERE WE PRODUCE LOVE AND JOY**

SCRIPTURE: JOHN 15

PART 1

CONTEXT

Before you begin your study, we will start with the context of the story we are about to read together: the setting, both cultural and historical; the people involved; and where our passage fits in the larger setting of Scripture. All these things help us make sense of what we're reading. Understanding the context of a Bible story is fundamental to reading Scripture well. Getting your bearings before you read will enable you to answer the question *What am I about to read?*

"AM I DECONSTRUCTING MY FAITH?"

I've been hearing this question a lot lately, from both men and women who are Christians. Although the question comes in different forms, these people share a common heartbeat in their self-examination. Far from walking away from their faith, they are experiencing a re-centering of Christ in their lives and a rebuilding of their faith practice. They are intentionally uncovering ways their faith is incongruent with Jesus and bravely taking steps to course correct.

But I understand why they're asking the question. I've asked myself similar things.

The common denominators in these conversations are comments like these:

- "I feel disconnected from a faith community."
- "I feel a divide between my beliefs and my actions."
- "I see incongruence between the words and behavior of other Christians."

- "I feel burned out and weary."
- "My joy is zapped."
- "The flourishing relationship I used to have with Christ is void of vibrancy and new growth."
- "My spiritual life is dormant."
- "Jesus feels distant."

Expressing this part of their faith journey is brave and, dare I say, full of faith and hope—faith in Jesus and hope that things can be different. Most of these people have a deep longing to stay connected to Jesus and to enjoy a flourishing faith. But that longing stands alongside a sobering reality that to stay connected and enjoy flourishing will mean resurrecting something that feels like it is dying or dead.

I wish that as I started having these conversations a few years ago I'd already read Matthew Sleeth's book *Reforesting Faith*. That's because in it he tells a story that could serve as metaphor for anyone who wants to commune with God but feels disconnected from him or his people—anyone who longs to bloom with new growth after a long season of what feels like death.[1]

In the 1960s, archaeologists excavated date seeds from Masada, the towering fortress of the Judean desert in the southern part of Israel. The archaeologists threw the date seeds, which are estimated to be thousands of years old, into a jar, which lay hidden for decades. In 2005, agricultural expert Elaine Solowey decided to replant the ancient seeds—and lo and behold, those date seeds took root and sprouted new growth.[2] They even produced fruit. The tree that grew out of the dormant seeds is called Methuselah.

Incredibly, "genetic tests indicate that Methuselah is most closely related to an ancient variety of date palm from Egypt known as Hayany, which fits with a legend that says dates came to Israel with the children of the Exodus, Solowey says."[3]

Methuselah's seeds were designed to grow where they are planted *even if that means breaking new ground and replanting in new places*. This is good news for those of us with faith the size of a tiny seed.

The tree imagery we're going to explore in this lesson is the True Vine, Jesus. Jesus chooses the image of a vine to teach us what it looks like to flourish. If the

> Being a branch to the true Vine means living with Christ, breathing with Christ, doing day-to-day life with Christ. It's the ongoing awareness of His presence, even when there's no feeling of His presence. Our lives become witness to His with-ness.[4]
>
> Beth Moore, *Chasing Vines*

ground you're planted in is cracked and dry, the True Vine invites you to connect deeply to him, the Source of Life.

What you are about to read is a sermon that Jesus preached to his closest friends and disciples just hours before his crucifixion. Some scholars call this section of Scripture a part of the Upper Room discourse. Emphasizing it so close to the end of his earthly ministry, Jesus positions this content as one of the most important things his disciples must remember in his absence.

Just moments after Jesus kneels down to wash his disciples' feet and then institutes the sacrament of Communion, Jesus' last words to his followers are about the joy of abiding in him. My prayer is that Jesus' words, familiar or not, would be a seedbed for new growth in your faith.

For those of us concerned about the replanting and regrowth we want in our relationship with Jesus, be encouraged. Jesus is our Cosmic Gardener. He knows the good soil, he has deep roots, and his water supply never runs dry.

Jesus knows how to grow anyone.

And when he produces fruit in our lives, it acts like love and feels like joy.

1. **PERSONAL CONTEXT: What is going on in your life right now that might impact how you understand this Bible passage?**

2. **SPIRITUAL CONTEXT: If you've never studied this passage before, what piques your curiosity? If you've studied this passage before, what impressions and insights do you recall? What problems or concerns might you have with the passage?**

SEEING

Seeing the text is vital if we want the heart of the Scripture passage to sink in. We read slowly and intentionally through the text with the context in mind. As we practice close, thoughtful reading of Scripture, we pick up on phrases, implications, and meanings we might otherwise have missed. Part 2 includes close Scripture reading and observation questions to empower you to answer the question *What is the story saying?*

1. **Read John 15:1-17 and circle every time Jesus uses the word *fruit*. (If you are the artistic type, you could use the margin to draw a tree and use the branches to connect every mention of fruit.)**

15 [Jesus said,] "I am the true vine, and my Father is the vinegrower. ² He removes every branch in me that bears no fruit. Every branch that bears fruit he prunes to make it bear more fruit. ³ You have already been cleansed by the word that I have spoken to you. ⁴ Abide in me as I abide in you. Just as the branch cannot bear fruit by itself unless it abides in the vine, neither can you unless you abide in me. ⁵ I am the vine, you are the branches. Those who abide in me and I in them bear much fruit, because apart from me you can do nothing. ⁶ Whoever does not abide in me is thrown away like a branch and withers; such branches are gathered, thrown into the fire, and burned. [7] If you abide in me, and my words abide in you, ask for whatever you wish, and it will be done for you. [8] My Father is glorified by this, that you bear much fruit and become my disciples. [9] As the Father has loved me, so I have loved you; abide in my love. [10] If you keep my commandments, you will abide in my love, just as I have kept my Father's commandments and abide in his love. [11] I have said these things to you so that my joy may be in you, and that your joy may be complete.

[12] "This is my commandment, that you love one another as I have loved you. [13] No one has greater love than this, to lay down one's life for one's friends. [14] You are my friends if you do what I command you. [15] I do not call you servants any longer, because the servant does not know what the master is doing; but I have called you friends, because I have made known to you everything that I have heard from my Father. [16] You did not choose me but I chose you. And I appointed you to go and bear fruit, fruit that will last, so that the Father will give you whatever you ask him in my name. [17] I am giving you these commands so that you may love one another."

JOHN 15:1-17

> John 15 is about living a naturally unexplainable life.[5]
>
> Beth Moore, *Chasing Vines*

2. When Jesus says he is the True Vine (John 15:1), what do you think he means?

Another word for *true* could be *authentic*. We see here that Jesus is authentic, which is an incredible reminder and encouragement for those of us wondering who is the real deal. Jesus' comments also suggest that there are vines who are not true or authentic. Sometimes we become so accustomed to fakeness it's hard to remember that Jesus is the bona fide Savior of the world. Only he is the growth agent to our seeds of faith, and only he has the power to sustain our growth.

3. **What does Jesus' speech reveal about God in John 15:1-2? List at least two observations.**

Our heavenly Father prunes us when we need purifying, preparing us to be more fruitful than we are right now. Fruit emerges because of the work of God and the power of Jesus in our lives. When the work of bearing fruit feels overwhelming or unlikely, remember who is tending to your care and supplying what you need. *The onus is not on you* to produce or create the fruit—you are simply called to bear, or bring forth, the fruit Jesus is creating in you.

4. **How does Jesus describe the branches that break off from the vine and wither (John 15:6)? What happens to those branches?**

In Jesus' farewell discourse to the disciples, he introduces the image of the vine and the branches (John 15:1-8). This metaphor differs from most of John's other christological images because it explicitly includes Jesus' disciples, who are pictured as the branches that must abide in the Vine in order to thrive and bear fruit.[6]

Richard B. Hays, *Echoes of Scripture in the Gospels*

5. How does this imagery connect to the elements of fire we saw at the Burning Bush and in the fires of Isaiah's prophecies?

As I write, two years into a global pandemic, our world is suffering through what some experts are calling "the Great Exhaustion."[7] Everyone is feeling the collective burden of living through such unprecedented times, and workplace resignations are at an all-time high.

In many of my casual conversations, I bring up the burnout I'm feeling—and I find solidarity in sharing my struggle because it seems that everyone else is struggling with burnout too. Even the language we use evokes the deeper feeling—of being used up and consumed, the ashy ruins of smoldering pieces of wood that are only good as kindling for fire.

This is not the flourishing life God has in mind for you and me. He knows we will face trials (John 16:33, NLT), and yet he still suggests that abiding is an option available to us in any circumstance. Only in abiding will we find the life we crave.

6. Look back at every time you circled the word *fruit* in John 15:1-17. What do you learn about the fruit Jesus is describing?

-

-

-

-

-

-

You and I were designed to bear fruit—to bear love that creates joy. A tall order, to be sure. How is love possible? How is a life full of joy an option? The key is to abide, staying close to Jesus, our True Vine.

Our English translations might use the word *abide* in Jesus' speech about the vine and branches, but in its original language of Greek, the word Jesus is using means "to remain" or "endure" or "wait."[8] It seems that part of staying close to Jesus is patiently waiting and enduring the tension waiting creates. But we don't abide or remain in vain—love is branching out in us when we abide in Jesus. As we stay connected to him, joy is finding its fulfillment in our lives.

UNDERSTANDING

Now that we've finished a close reading of the Scriptures, we're going to spend some time on interpretation: doing our best to understand what God was saying to the original audience and what he's teaching us through the process. But to do so, we need to learn his ways and consider how God's Word would have been understood by the original audience before apply-ing the same truths to our own lives. "Scripture interpretation" may sound a little stuffy, but understanding what God means to communicate to us in the Bible is crucial to enjoying a close relationship with Jesus. Part 3 will enable you to answer the question *What does it mean?*

WHEN JESUS SAYS HE IS THE TRUE VINE in John 15, this is an audacious claim that the original audience would have been shocked by. Any first-century Jew would have heard those words and immediately thought of Psalm 80: an ancient song about God, the Rescuer, bringing Israel out of Egypt.

1. **Circle any time you see the word *vine*, *branches*, or *fruit* in Psalm 80:8–19.**

   ⁸ You brought a vine out of Egypt;

       you drove out the nations and planted it.

   ⁹ You cleared the ground for it;

       it took deep root and filled the land.

   ¹⁰ The mountains were covered with its shade,

       the mighty cedars with its branches;

¹¹ it sent out its branches to the sea,

and its shoots to the River.

¹² Why then have you broken down its walls,

so that all who pass along the way pluck its fruit?

¹³ The boar from the forest ravages it,

and all that move in the field feed on it.

¹⁴ Turn again, O God of hosts;

look down from heaven, and see;

have regard for this vine,

¹⁵ the stock that your right hand planted.

¹⁶ They have burned it with fire, they have cut it down;

may they perish at the rebuke of your countenance.

¹⁷ But let your hand be upon the one at your right hand,

the one whom you made strong for yourself.

¹⁸ Then we will never turn back from you;

give us life, and we will call on your name.

¹⁹ Restore us, O Lᴏʀᴅ God of hosts;

let your face shine, that we may be saved.

PSALM 80:8-19

In the Old Testament, the people devoted to the God of the Israelites believed Israel was the vine coming out of Egypt. Israel was the stump or root planted in the Promised Land to flourish and grow. Israel would branch out and bloom where they'd been planted. When Jesus announces that he is the True Vine, he is "daring to supplant Israel."[9]

In Jesus' day, everybody knew what the vine represented: Israel, plain and simple.[10]

Beth Moore, *Chasing Vines*

---

2. **According to Psalm 80:14-16, what was evidence that Israel was undergoing God's judgment for turning their back on God?**

Israel, the vine of the Old Testament, does not remain faithful to God—and as a consequence, the nation is treated like withering branches that are burned with fire. When Jesus preaches that he is the True Vine, he is alluding to Psalm 80 and several other passages in the Old Testament that vividly describe tree imagery.

3. **What do you think Jesus meant when he said he was the True Vine? Check all that you might consider to be true.**

   ☐ Jesus is better than Israel.

   ☐ Jesus is the embodiment of Israel.

   ☐ Jesus fulfills Israel's calling.

JESUS AS THE EMBODIMENT OF ISRAEL

Israel	Jesus
Israel was called by God to live an obedient life.	Jesus is the embodiment of Israel living in perfect obedience to God.
Israel faced divine judgment as a nation.	Jesus willingly chose to suffer divine judgment: the Cross.
Israel experienced exile at the hands of the Assyrians and Babylonians.	Jesus willingly chose to be forsaken by God, exiled to the grave for three days.
Israel was restored—time and time again—to God.	Jesus was restored to new life and resurrected from the dead.
Israel always had a remnant survive God's judgment.	Jesus gave birth to the New Testament church, or a New Testament remnant of God's faithful people, to inherit God's promises to his people.

> The Evangelist John . . . transforms the image of the vine into a christological symbol. Just as Jesus embodies the true meaning of Israel's temple and its religious festivals, so also he now becomes "the true Vine" (John 15:1), the figural fulfillment of the nation's identity and its hopes.[11]
>
> Richard B. Hays, *Echoes of Scripture in the Gospels*

4. What implications would Jesus' words in John 15 have for the Jewish listeners?

5. How do Jesus' words impact you as a Christ follower?

MAKING CONNECTIONS

An important part of understanding the meaning of a Bible passage is getting a sense of its place in the broader storyline of Scripture. When we make connections between different parts of the Bible, we get a glimpse of the unity and cohesion of the Scriptures.

Every tree we've studied together represents a decision tree. Whether it has been the trees in the Garden of Eden, the Burning Bush (Tree) at Sinai, or the tree imagery in Isaiah's prophecies about the Messiah Tree, all these Bible passages have a unifying pattern. Each tree becomes a test where God's people have to make hard choices:

Choices to trust that God will give wisdom instead of taking wisdom into our own hands. Choices to trust God as our Rescuer instead of listening to the oppressive voices of tyrants. Choices to remain faithful to God instead of embracing idols.

Before we move on to respond to Jesus' teachings in John 15, I want to connect the True Vine sermon to the Garden of Eden. While the Garden of Eden trees symbolize a test about which fruit we will consume, the True Vine test in John 15 is about which fruit we will produce. In Eden the fruit created a decision tree: to either pick and consume fruit that would lead to wisdom—to choose God's way—or to take wisdom into our own hands and be separated from him. In John 15, during Jesus' sermon, the issue is whether we will produce good, lasting fruit or become like withered firewood, consumed by the flames of fire.

The good news for us is that producing fruit that lasts doesn't depend on our own excellence. Remember—we're not the vine. We're branches. When we are connected to the True Vine, receiving nutrients and life from him, we can't help but bear fruit.

6. **What kind of fruit do we bear as we connect to our Source? Let's check out Galatians 5:22-23.**

   22 The fruit of the Spirit is love, joy, peace, forbearance, kindness, goodness, faithfulness, 23 gentleness and self-control. Against such things there is no law.

   GALATIANS 5:22-23, NIV

7. **Consider your actions and interactions this week. What kind of fruit are you bearing as you move through the world? What fruit do you want to see more of in your life?**

8. What keeps you connected to the life-giving sustenance of the True Vine?

— — —

Let's take a look at our Sticks Storyline now that we've added in the True Vine.

THE STICKS STORYLINE OF SCRIPTURE

Stick(s)	Element of Fire	The Decision
the Tree of Life & the Tree of the Knowledge of Good and Evil (Genesis 2–3)	Flaming swords of the cherubim guard the Garden of Eden after the exile.	Will we choose to live wisely with wisdom from God or try to take matters into our own hands?
the Burning Bush (Exodus 3)	The Sinai tree/bush is in flames but is not consumed.	Will we take notice when God is trying get our attention or ignore his voice and keep moving on?
the Messiah Tree (Isaiah 1, 6, 11, 53)	The smoke in the Temple and the flaming coals burn with heat from the fire.	Will we branch out from our shady family trees and grow deep roots in God's family?
the True Vine, Jesus (John 15)	The branches who do not abide in Jesus wither and are used as firewood.	Will we stay connected to Jesus for a fruitful life or try to produce good fruit on our own?
the Tree of Life (Revelation 22)	If you choose to live outside the Garden City gates, you will be cast into a lake of fire.	Will we choose to reframe our perspective or follow old patterns?

Fear Response	Consequences of the Wrong Choice	Wise Choice
Adam and Eve hide from God between the trees out of fear and shame.	When Adam and Eve choose to seek wisdom for themselves, they end up exiled from Eden.	Trust God to give us wisdom through an ongoing relationship with him.
Moses hides his face from God at the Burning Bush out of fear.	If the Israelites don't choose to follow Moses in the Exodus, they will remain in Egypt as slaves and exiles.	Notice, listen to, and trust God's voice when he's trying to get our attention.
The prophet Isaiah asks God how long his judgment will last, fearing none will survive.	Since the Israelites choose idolatry, God allows them to be exiled from Jerusalem and enslaved to the Babylonians and Assyrians.	Remain faithful to God, knowing he's always going to be faithful to us.
Jesus quickly encourages his followers that his friendship and love for them does not waver, as if he knows his words will cause fear.	Those who do not choose to abide in Christ will be exiled to fire, where all efforts will be consumed and reduced to ashes.	Stay close to Jesus to bear good fruit.
There will be no more fear in the new heaven and new earth.	If we do not choose to follow Christ, the Tree of Life, we will be exiled to the lake of fire.	Choose to live near the Tree of Life.

1. What choice are you facing right now? How can you pay attention to where God is at work?

2. What did you learn about God's character in this lesson?

3. How should these truths shape your faith community and change you?

RESPONDING

The purpose of Bible study is to help you become more Christlike; that's why part 4 will include journaling space for your reflection on and responses to the content and a blank checklist for actionable next steps. You'll be able to process what you're learning so that you can live out the concepts and pursue Christlikeness. Part 4 will enable you to answer the questions *What truths is this passage teaching?* and *How do I apply this to my life?*

I RARELY SHOP IN GROCERY STORES ANYMORE because food-delivery apps are one of my favorite technological advancements. With a few taps on my phone, I can order groceries or send a friend a meal while I'm on a conference call for work.

My only complaint with online grocery shopping is that it's tough to get the produce just right. Everything else on my shopping list is packaged, which means the product I'm getting is consistent. If I buy a frozen pizza, I know what I am going to receive because all the pizzas are manufactured the same. If I order Honey Nut Cheerios, I know there won't be any variance in the product that gets delivered to my door. But produce is a whole other story.

In our house we joke that avocados are the butter of Mexico—and we love butter. We probably go through nine avocados as a family in one week. But we always insist on buying our avocados in person to ensure the quality. If I tried to type into the grocery app all the ways I need the shopper to check the avocados, it would be an embarrassingly long list of questions:

- What exactly is the shade of the avocado?
- How firmly are you pressing into it?
- When you're pressing gently, how much does the avocado indent?
- Is the tip still intact?
- Are there any cracks in the skin?
- Is it large enough to spoon out of but small enough so that it doesn't go to waste once it's cut?
- And could you please get three that are really firm, three that are medium firm, and three that need to be eaten today?

I know. It's a lot. I'd rather just have someone in our family make a trip to the grocery store to inspect the butter of Mexico ourselves. If you're an avocado-toast person, you get me right now. And you banana lovers can also relate.

You've got to check your fruit. The personal shoppers can sling the gallons of Blue Bell and smoosh my frozen pizzas into the crevices of the shopping cart, but for the love of Mexico, do not bruise my avocados.

In our faith, checking our own fruit is crucial too. What is being produced in us? What does that fruit reveal about us? How can we ensure that our fruit is the produce we want?

The relationship of mutual abiding that Jesus calls for is not a relationship of equals, or of equal contributions: Jesus' indwelling makes abiding and obedience possible because he is the life of the Father given to the branches.

Strikingly, Jesus does not exhort his disciples to bear fruit; rather, he exhorts his disciples to remain attached to him, the source of life.[12]

Marianne Meye Thompson, *John*

If we desire an abundant, fruitful, flourishing life, we've got to check our spiritual fruit. Jesus assures us that if we abide in him, he will produce in us lasting, good fruit. How do we know he is the One cultivating it? Because it will act like love and feel like joy.

1. CHECK YOUR FRUIT FOR THE LOVE.

One piece of evidence that we are abiding in Jesus is that we will love one another as he has loved us (John 15:12). When we stay connected to Jesus, our friends will describe us as loving. Our neighbors will see us as loving. The words coming out of our mouths, even about the people getting on our nerves, will be loving. Our instinct will be to love the people around us. Our thoughts toward others will be like the love described in the Bible in 1 Corinthians 13: patient and kind.

If we inspect the fruit of our lives and find envy, rudeness, resentment, or anger, the fruit is not coming from Jesus. Maybe it's coming from trauma or the hurt we carry in our hearts. Maybe it comes from selfishness or unawareness. Whatever the case may be, we need to check our fruit for love. And if love is missing, the fruit doesn't belong to Jesus. When we snap at a loved one, or overreact to stress, or act uncharitably, we can be sure the source of that produce isn't Christ.

The good news is that we don't have to produce love in our own lives—that's Jesus' job. He is the producer of love. We simply bear what he is cultivating in our lives. If you find that your fruit isn't loving, ask Jesus to bring you closer to him and help you establish new behaviors.

2. CHECK YOUR FRUIT FOR THE JOY.

I'm sure my licensed professional counselor would have some thoughts on why I feel burdened by the True Vine sermon. As I internalize Jesus' words, I feel comfort but also conviction. As I check my fruit, I'm realizing that I lack joy. I have so much room to grow in joy, and I feel helpless to create the change I want in my life. Which leads to a shame cycle: *Why can't I be more joyful on my own?*

You know the answer. I can't do it on my own because I'm not supposed to. Joy is a product of God at work in my life, not of me trying harder. Jesus calls us to abide and bear fruit, not to produce it ourselves. But alas, my default mode isn't waiting on God's effective gardening in my heart—it's trying to conjure up joy myself. You can imagine how this line of thinking can smoosh the joy right out of my heart like it's a pressed avocado.

But Jesus says, "I have said these things to you so that my joy may be in you, and that your joy may be complete" (John 15:11). Jesus invites us to stay close to him, and one of the surest ways we can diagnose whether we're doing that is to check our lives for joy. If the joy is missing, we might be abiding in our own self-effort rather than in Jesus' abundant, life-giving ways.

Use this journaling space to process what you are learning.

Ask yourself how these truths impact your relationship with God and with others.

What is the Holy Spirit bringing to your mind as actionable next steps in your faith journey?

-

-

-

LESSON FIVE

REFRAMING YOUR PERSPECTIVE
WITH VIEWS FROM THE TREETOPS

THE TREE OF LIFE:
WHERE GOD'S GLORY REDEEMS ALL THINGS

SCRIPTURE: REVELATION 22

PART 1

CONTEXT

Before you begin your study, we will start with the context of the story we are about to read together: the setting, both cultural and historical; the people involved; and where our passage fits in the larger setting of Scripture. All these things help us make sense of what we're reading. Understanding the context of a Bible story is fundamental to reading Scripture well. Getting your bearings before you read will enable you to answer the question *What am I about to read?*

FOR THE LAST TWENTY YEARS, the Dallas Arboretum has been my sanctuary—my Eden. Tucked around White Rock Lake, right in the middle of the city, the magnificent garden is brimming with blooms. Somehow the staff manages to grow season-appropriate plants all year long in the most intricate, creative patterns. Everywhere you turn, the artistry takes your breath away.

My arboretum visits started while I was a student at Dallas Theological Seminary. When I needed to escape the busy city, looming deadlines, or the chaos of life, I'd make a trip. As soon as I stepped into the garden, the hustle and hurry slowed long enough for me to reframe my burdens. I can always count on my perspective shifting as I mosey through the Arboretum.

The last tree we will study together has the power to completely alter your perspective on your present circumstances. Much like me on my trips to the Dallas Arboretum, we are about to take an adventure into a new world. Our journey will be through the eyes of John, the beloved disciple of Jesus and the author of the last book in the Bible, Revelation.

John has an encounter with God that lifts him into the heavenly realms with a vision of the future. With narrative imagery that has captivated Christians for centuries, the book of Revelation describes a symbolic world that centers the Tree of Life in a new, cosmic, Garden City—a new Jerusalem. It is the same Tree of Life that is centered in the Garden of Eden in the book of Genesis. As bookends of the Holy Scriptures, both Genesis and Revelation hinge on a sacred tree. The Tree of Life is, again, a decision tree. A place where you and I must resolve ourselves with faithful determination to choose wise living.

The book of Revelation can be confusing because of all the symbols and double meanings. But one thing we know for sure is the political and social context in which John was writing this letter: The Roman Empire was the dominating force in the world. Rome had positioned itself as sovereign, religiously and politically. But the subversive message John advances in the book of Revelation is that God is on his throne; he alone is sovereign. God has all the power. God reigns universally, unthreatened by any earthly powers. No matter what mess Rome was causing in the world, God offers this enduring hope— the fruition of redemption is coming and will conquer evil once and for all.

> Revelation is the unveiling of the way the world looks when viewed through the eyes of God.[1]
>
> Gail R. O'Day, "Revelation," in *Theological Bible Commentary*

In context, the Book of Revelation is not just an apocalyptic vision or apostolic letter or piece of prophetic literature but a new way of seeing our world. It is a vision of our future but also a reimagining of our present through the lens of hope.

What you are about to read is the last chapter of the Bible, Revelation 22. You're about to see that what God started in the Garden he completes in a new Garden City. God's project—to see all of us flourish and live forever near the Tree of Life—is finally realized.

My prayer is that you will feel the relief. That you will exclaim with me: *Finally!*

Revelation is grounded in John's central theological conviction that no power on heaven or earth can negate the fulfillment of God's hopes for creation.[2]

Gail R. O'Day, "Revelation," in *Theological Bible Commentary*

1. **PERSONAL CONTEXT: What is going on in your life right now that might impact how you understand this Bible passage?**

2. **SPIRITUAL CONTEXT: If you've never studied this passage before, what piques your curiosity? If you've studied this passage before, what impressions and insights do you recall? What problems or concerns might you have with the passage?**

PART 2

SEEING

Seeing the text is vital if we want the heart of the Scripture passage to sink in. We read slowly and intentionally through the text with the context in mind. As we practice close, thoughtful reading of Scripture, we pick up on phrases, implications, and meanings we might otherwise have missed. Part 2 includes close Scripture reading and observation questions to empower you to answer the question *What is the story saying?*

1. **Read Revelation 22:1-21 and box the words *tree of life* anytime you see the phrase.**

22 Then the angel showed me the river of the water of life, bright as crystal, flowing from the throne of God and of the Lamb ² through the middle of the street of the city. On either side of the river is the tree of life with its twelve kinds of fruit, producing its fruit each month; and the leaves of the tree are for the healing of the nations. ³ Nothing accursed will be found there any more. But the throne of God and of the Lamb will be in it, and his servants will worship him; ⁴ they will see his face, and his name will be on their foreheads. ⁵ And there will be no more night; they need no light of lamp or sun, for the Lord God will be their light, and they will reign forever and ever.

⁶ And he said to me, "These words are trustworthy and true, for the Lord, the God of the spirits of the prophets, has sent his angel to show his servants what must soon take place."

⁷ "See, I am coming soon! Blessed is the one who keeps the words of the prophecy of this book."

⁸ I, John, am the one who heard and saw these things. And when I heard and saw them, I fell down to worship at the feet of the angel who showed them to me; ⁹ but he said to me, "You must not do that! I am a fellow servant with you and your comrades the prophets, and with those who keep the words of this book. Worship God!"

¹⁰ And he said to me, "Do not seal up the words of the prophecy of this book, for the time is near. ¹¹ Let the evildoer still do evil, and the filthy still be filthy, and the righteous still do right, and the holy still be holy."

¹² "See, I am coming soon; my reward is with me, to repay according to everyone's work. ¹³ I am the Alpha and the Omega, the first and the last, the beginning and the end."

¹⁴ Blessed are those who wash their robes, so that they will have the right to the tree of life and may enter the city by the gates. ¹⁵ Outside are the dogs and sorcerers and fornicators and murderers and idolaters, and everyone who loves and practices falsehood.

¹⁶ "It is I, Jesus, who sent my angel to you with this testimony for the churches. I am the root and the descendant of David, the bright morning star."

¹⁷ The Spirit and the bride say, "Come."
And let everyone who hears say, "Come."
And let everyone who is thirsty come.
Let anyone who wishes take the water of life as a gift.

¹⁸ I warn everyone who hears the words of the prophecy of this book: if anyone adds to them, God will add to that person the plagues described in this book; ¹⁹ if anyone takes away from the words of the book of this

prophecy, God will take away that person's share in the tree of life and in the holy city, which are described in this book.

²⁰ The one who testifies to these things says, "Surely I am coming soon."

Amen. Come, Lord Jesus!

²¹ The grace of the Lord Jesus be with all the saints. Amen.

REVELATION 22:1-21

2. What is the purpose of the leaves from the Tree of Life, according to Revelation 22:2?

As I finished writing this lesson, Russia invaded Ukraine. The world has felt so fragile lately, and I'm acutely aware of our need for peace. Every nation, including the one I live in, needs to be healed by God. If Russia's cruelty has proven anything, it is that humanity needs to be rescued. All I can think about are the leaves from the Tree of Life and how we need them right now. The chaos of the world makes John's testimony all the more hopeful—because he says God is coming soon.

3. According to Revelation 22:14, who has the right to the Tree of Life?

In each story with tree imagery, we've studied an element of holiness—where people are purified in God's presence or respond to God's presence in holy reverence. Our final tree is no different. Approaching the Tree of Life requires holiness.

What exactly does John mean when he says, "Blessed are those who wash their robes" (Revelation 22:14)? Scholar Brian K. Blount explains: "The blood of

Christ is the detergent that launders those robes to be dazzling clean."[3] He goes on to say that washing the robes is "a metaphor for witnessing, which is, in the context of chapter 22, the work that merits the reward Christ offers."[4]

4. How does Jesus identify himself in Revelation 22:16?

Jesus is like a Cosmic Tree, illuminating the whole Garden City. As the source of light and life, Jesus is the root of David, the One everyone has been hoping for. Jesus is the Tree of Life—the life source and nourishment everyone needs.

5. Write out what Revelation 22:19 says could jeopardize someone's access to the Tree of Life.

The stakes are high at this decision tree. Choosing to ignore or remove parts of this prophecy is tantamount to choosing an eternity separated from Christ, the Tree of Life.

The hopeful future John's vision portrays could help us reframe our present circumstances. If your life has been chipping away at your confidence in God's compassion or power, hang with me as we explore how John's vision in Revelation is a continuation of God's plan that started in the Old Testament. If you're thinking Jesus can't come soon enough, keep reading.

UNDERSTANDING

Now that we've finished a close reading of the Scriptures, we're going to spend some time on interpretation: doing our best to understand what God was saying to the original audience and what he's teaching us through the process. But to do so, we need to learn his ways and consider how God's Word would have been understood by the original audience before applying the same truths to our own lives. "Scripture interpretation" may sound a little stuffy, but understanding what God means to communicate to us in the Bible is crucial to enjoying a close relationship with Jesus. Part 3 will enable you to answer the question *What does it mean?*

TO TRULY UNDERSTAND the last chapter in the Bible and the deeper implications surrounding the Tree of Life in the new Jerusalem, we need to review what happened right before in John's vision. Here's what John had to say.

1. **Read Revelation 21:1-14, 22-26. In the margin, number everything that will *not* be present in the new Jerusalem.**

21 Then I saw a new heaven and a new earth; for the first heaven and the first earth had passed away, and the sea was no more. ² And I saw the holy city, the new Jerusalem, coming down out of heaven from God, prepared as a bride adorned for her husband. ³ And I heard a loud voice from the throne saying,

"See, the home of God is among mortals.
    He will dwell with them as their God;
    they will be his peoples,
    and God himself will be with them;
    [4] he will wipe every tear from their eyes.
    Death will be no more;
    mourning and crying and pain will be no more,
    for the first things have passed away."

[5] And the one who was seated on the throne said, "See, I am making all things new." Also he said, "Write this, for these words are trustworthy and true." [6] Then he said to me, "It is done! I am the Alpha and the Omega, the beginning and the end. To the thirsty I will give water as a gift from the spring of the water of life. [7] Those who conquer will inherit these things, and I will be their God and they will be my children. [8] But as for the cowardly, the faithless, the polluted, the murderers, the fornicators, the sorcerers, the idolaters, and all liars, their place will be in the lake that burns with fire and sulfur, which is the second death."

[9] Then one of the seven angels who had the seven bowls full of the seven last plagues came and said to me, "Come, I will show you the bride, the wife of the Lamb." [10] And in the spirit he carried me away to a great, high mountain and showed me the holy city Jerusalem coming down out of heaven from God. [11] It has the glory of God and a radiance like a very rare jewel, like jasper, clear as crystal. [12] It has a great, high wall with twelve gates, and at the gates twelve angels, and on the gates are inscribed the names of the twelve tribes of the Israelites; [13] on the

east three gates, on the north three gates, on the south three gates, and on the west three gates. ¹⁴ And the wall of the city has twelve foundations, and on them are the twelve names of the twelve apostles of the Lamb. . . .

²² I saw no temple in the city, for its temple is the Lord God the Almighty and the Lamb. ²³ And the city has no need of sun or moon to shine on it, for the glory of God is its light, and its lamp is the Lamb. ²⁴ The nations will walk by its light, and the kings of the earth will bring their glory into it. ²⁵ Its gates will never be shut by day—and there will be no night there. ²⁶ People will bring into it the glory and the honor of the nations.

REVELATION 21:1-14, 22-26

2. **Reflecting back on what we learned about Roman imperialism (in part 1), how is the new Jerusalem different from the world in which Christians were living during the time John wrote Revelation?**

Like his prophetic forebears, John offers future visions that have a present ethical purpose. He declares what will, or perhaps better said in this apocalyptic setting, what *must* be, so that those who hear and read his words, knowing the landscape of the future, will direct their lives in ways that conduct them toward a beneficent engagement with that future.⁶

Brian K. Blount, *Revelation*

3. **Consider your own experience. How will the new Jerusalem be different from the world in which you live right now?**

John's vision of our future weaves together several luminous threads of God's glory. As the new Jerusalem comes down from heaven to earth, death is defeated and the evils of the Roman Empire feel small. Pause and reflect on these truths for a moment. If what we are reading is true—and I believe it is—our future as Christ followers includes a reality where evil is no more. Death will be dead. Every single sinful, evil, harmful circumstance will not only cease but will also have its power taken away—and by God's grace, redeemed. How? I'm not sure. We will have to wait and see it with our own eyes. But don't let the "how" distract you from the fact that God is going to wipe away all your tears and redeem everything that caused them.

> With the death of death, access to the tree of life is restored.[7]
>
> **Leland Ryken, James C. Wilhoit, and Tremper Longman III, eds.,** *Dictionary of Biblical Imagery*

4. **What are some things in your life that cause you to shed tears right now?**

5. Describe a time when your perspective shifted. What changed your mind? How did the new perspective change the way you live now?

6. How should John's vision of your future alter your perspective of your present circumstances? How would your life be different if you viewed your life through this lens of hope?

Don't miss the fact that John's vision now gives us all an opportunity to decide if we want to live in this future city, washed by Christ's blood and with access to the Tree of Life, or if we want to die in our sins without access to our Source of Life. This new perspective John offers us on our future should impact our present. Although we continue to live in a broken, fallen world, we should live with our eyes on the horizon. Hope is up ahead. Even as we mourn the war and pain and sickness of now, we rest within the truth that this is not the end of the story.

MAKING CONNECTIONS

An important part of understanding the meaning of a Bible passage is getting a sense of its place in the broader storyline of Scripture. When we make connections between different parts of the Bible, we get a glimpse of the unity and cohesion of the Scriptures.

Why is the Tree of Life now available to human beings, after we saw humanity separated from it at the beginning of time? The answer lies with another tree. Let's read together from 1 Peter 2:24-25:

> [24] He himself bore our sins in his body on the tree, that we may cease from sinning and live for righteousness. By his wounds you were healed. [25] For you were going astray like sheep but now you have turned back to the shepherd and guardian of your souls.
>
> 1 PETER 2:24-25, NET

7. How does Jesus' death on a tree connect to the Tree of Life?

8. Why do you think the imagery of a cross, or a broken tree, was important to include in the Scriptures?

In Revelation the tree of life is the supreme image of future splendor and paradise regained. Its final appearance in the Bible occurs in the last chapter, as part of the combined city and garden that climaxes the heavenly vision.[8]

Leland Ryken, James C. Wilhoit, and Tremper Longman III, eds., *Dictionary of Biblical Imagery*

Because of his death on a tree and his resurrection in a garden, Jesus is the Tree of Life for all who choose to follow him. We are given the same choice Adam and Eve were given all the way back in the Garden of Eden: Will we trust in our own wisdom, or will we choose the life that is offered to us? Throughout Scripture this decision branches out, showing us time and again what happens when we choose life—and what happens when we don't. And it all culminates in the Garden City's Cosmic Tree in the last book of the Bible, Revelation.

— — —

Let's complete the Sticks Storyline.

THE STICKS STORYLINE OF SCRIPTURE

Stick(s)	Element of Fire	The Decision
the Tree of Life & the Tree of the Knowledge of Good and Evil (Genesis 2–3)	Flaming swords of the cherubim guard the Garden of Eden after the exile.	Will we choose to live wisely with wisdom from God or try to take matters into our own hands?
the Burning Bush (Exodus 3)	The Sinai tree/bush is in flames but is not consumed.	Will we take notice when God is trying get our attention or ignore his voice and keep moving on?
the Messiah Tree (Isaiah 1, 6, 11, 53)	The smoke in the Temple and the flaming coals burn with heat from the fire.	Will we branch out from our shady family trees and grow deep roots in God's family?
the True Vine, Jesus (John 15)	The branches who do not abide in Jesus wither and are used as firewood.	Will we stay connected to Jesus for a fruitful life or try to produce good fruit on our own?
the Tree of Life (Revelation 22)	If you choose to live outside the Garden City gates, you will be cast into a lake of fire.	Will we choose to reframe our perspective or follow old patterns?

Fear Response	Consequences of the Wrong Choice	Wise Choice
Adam and Eve hide from God between the trees out of fear and shame.	When Adam and Eve choose to seek wisdom for themselves, they end up exiled from Eden.	Trust God to give us wisdom through an ongoing relationship with him.
Moses hides his face from God at the Burning Bush out of fear.	If the Israelites don't choose to follow Moses in the Exodus, they will remain in Egypt as slaves and exiles.	Notice, listen to, and trust God's voice when he's trying to get our attention.
The prophet Isaiah asks God how long his judgment will last, fearing none will survive.	Since the Israelites choose idolatry, God allows them to be exiled from Jerusalem and enslaved to the Babylonians and Assyrians.	Remain faithful to God, knowing he's always going to be faithful to us.
Jesus quickly encourages his followers that his friendship and love for them does not waver, as if he knows his words will cause fear.	Those who do not choose to abide in Christ will be exiled to fire, where all efforts will be consumed and reduced to ashes.	Stay close to Jesus to bear good fruit.
There will be no more fear in the new heaven and new earth.	If we do not choose to follow Christ, the Tree of Life, we will be exiled to the lake of fire.	Choose to live near the Tree of Life.

1. What choice are you facing right now? How can you pay attention to where God is at work?

2. What did you learn about God's character in this lesson?

3. How should these truths shape your faith community and change you?

PART 4

RESPONDING

The purpose of Bible study is to help you become more Christlike; that's why part 4 will include journaling space for your reflection on and responses to the content and a blank checklist for actionable next steps. You'll be able to process what you're learning so that you can live out the concepts and pursue Christlikeness. Part 4 will enable you to answer the questions *What truths is this passage teaching?* and *How do I apply this to my life?*

I'VE WATCHED THE SUN RISE AND SET countless times at the Dallas Arboretum, always from the same spot in the garden: the large hill overlooking White Rock Lake. As you gaze toward the horizon, you can see a whole host of treetops. There is something special about seeing the big picture of the city of Dallas from the viewpoint of this Arboretum hill. It puts everything in perspective.

My favorite part of watching the sun rise at the Arboretum is that magical moment when the first rays of sunlight are bursting forth from the earth's skyline. For a few minutes the expanse of the sky and the earth down below are connected by the sunbeams, and heaven feels a little closer to earth.

As I've studied Revelation 22 and the Tree of Life in the new Garden City, I've felt the same way I do when I see an Arboretum sunrise—hopeful and peaceful, knowing we have hope on our horizon. Soon enough, Jesus is coming back to set our world right. He's going to complete what he started in the Garden of Eden, and he will be our Tree of Life in the Garden City. According to John's vision in Revelation, when we live in the Garden City, we will experience what it was like to live in Eden, with the Tree of Life illuminating and sustaining us all.

As we wrap up our study of trees in the Bible storyline, here are two ways you can respond to the Tree of Life in the Garden City.

1. REFRAME YOUR PERSPECTIVE THROUGH THE LENS OF HOPE.

Whatever it is that creates a shame cycle in your life is coming to an end. Whatever sin struggle you feel stuck in right now will no longer exist in the new heaven and earth. Whatever harm has been done to you or to others, that's going to be redeemed in the new heaven and new earth. Whatever healing you've been waiting on—the healing from a broken relationship, dreams unrealized, hope lost—healing is coming soon! No doctor or medication or treatment can heal like Jesus in the new Garden City. One leaf from the Tree of Life, and you will be healed. Our nations will be healed too. The unreconcilable differences and divides fracturing the body of Christ and creating wedges in our relationships will be made whole in Jesus. Evil has an end. There is coming a day when it will perish under God's judgment. When it feels like evil is multiplying in our world or that the enemy is winning—remember, this is not how our story ends. The whole world will fully experience God's absolute, unthreatened power when Jesus returns. He will rule our world with justice and mercy, realized wholly and completely as we've never seen before.

> John shows the future of an eschatological relationship with God—pictured as a new Jerusalem—and what that relationship requires so that people can act now in ways that will enable them to participate in such a relationship then.[9]
>
> Brian K. Blount, *Revelation*

2. PRACTICE LIVING HOPEFULLY.

You know what might hold us back from reframing our present through the lens of a hopeful future? You and I are so practiced at living disappointed. I'd love to blame the global pandemic or the fears of World War III, but the truth is that life in general can be disappointing at times. The more our dreams are dashed and our hopes deferred, we start to look skeptically at joy and roll our eyes at optimism. I think we might all be afraid to believe the future will be better. Notice that I didn't say it only *might* be better. Based on what we studied together in Revelation 22, we *know* it will be better.

But with the disappointment around us, we can't just decide in one moment to be more expectant. We're going to have to *make this choice daily*, sometimes moment by moment. It will take practice, and we will never get it perfect, but we can embrace our future hope and let it be our vantage point for the present.

Use this journaling space to process what you are learning.

Ask yourself how these truths impact your relationship with God and with others.

What is the Holy Spirit bringing to your mind as actionable next steps in your faith journey?

-

-

-

As You Go

YOU DID IT. You studied five places in the Bible where a tree, bush, or vine is the focal point: the Tree of Life and Tree of the Knowledge of Good and Evil, the Burning Bush (or Tree), the Messiah Tree in Isaiah's prophecies, the True Vine in John 15, and the Tree of Life again in Revelation 22. All five places with tree imagery share several key elements:

- the sacred echoes of fire,
- the tendency for God's people to be afraid when they have to make hard choices,
- the element of exile as one of the consequences presented at our decision trees, and
- the hope of what happens when we choose to live into the sustaining power of God.

These stand-out elements link together a cohesive storyline:

THE STICKS STORYLINE OF SCRIPTURE

Stick(s)	Element of Fire	The Decision
the Tree of Life & the Tree of the Knowledge of Good and Evil (Genesis 2–3)	Flaming swords of the cherubim guard the Garden of Eden after the exile.	Will we choose to live wisely with wisdom from God or try to take matters into our own hands?
the Burning Bush (Exodus 3)	The Sinai tree/bush is in flames but is not consumed.	Will we take notice when God is trying get our attention or ignore his voice and keep moving on?
the Messiah Tree (Isaiah 1, 6, 11, 53)	The smoke in the Temple and the flaming coals burn with heat from the fire.	Will we branch out from our shady family trees and grow deep roots in God's family?
the True Vine, Jesus (John 15)	The branches who do not abide in Jesus wither and are used as firewood.	Will we stay connected to Jesus for a fruitful life or try to produce good fruit on our own?
the Tree of Life (Revelation 22)	If you choose to live outside the Garden City gates, you will be cast into a lake of fire.	Will we choose to reframe our perspective or follow old patterns?

Fear Response	Consequences of the Wrong Choice	Wise Choice
Adam and Eve hide from God between the trees out of fear and shame.	When Adam and Eve choose to seek wisdom for themselves, they end up exiled from Eden.	Trust God to give us wisdom through an ongoing relationship with him.
Moses hides his face from God at the Burning Bush out of fear.	If the Israelites don't choose to follow Moses in the Exodus, they will remain in Egypt as slaves and exiles.	Notice, listen to, and trust God's voice when he's trying to get our attention.
The prophet Isaiah asks God how long his judgment will last, fearing none will survive.	Since the Israelites choose idolatry, God allows them to be exiled from Jerusalem and enslaved to the Babylonians and Assyrians.	Remain faithful to God, knowing he's always going to be faithful to us.
Jesus quickly encourages his followers that his friendship and love for them does not waver, as if he knows his words will cause fear.	Those who do not choose to abide in Christ will be exiled to fire, where all efforts will be consumed and reduced to ashes.	Stay close to Jesus to bear good fruit.
There will be no more fear in the new heaven and new earth.	If we do not choose to follow Christ, the Tree of Life, we will be exiled to the lake of fire.	Choose to live near the Tree of Life.

With every story with tree imagery, I hope God reminded you that he will help you through hard choices. He will sustain and empower you as you rely on his power, strength, and direction. As you face the countless decisions of life, he promises to give you his wisdom so that you can live wisely and honor him. This is possible because he offers himself to us as the Source of wisdom.

PS: I've loved this journey with you, and I hope you join me again—this time, for the *Stones* study.

Each **Storyline Bible Study** is five lessons long and can be paired with its thematic partner for a seamless ten-week study. Complement the *Sticks* study with

STONES
MAKING GOD'S FAITHFULNESS
THE BEDROCK OF YOUR FAITH

The *Stones* Bible study will guide you through five stone-related stories because stones are physical reminders of God's faithful activity in the lives of his people.

LESSON ONE: Your Worthiness Comes from God's Faithfulness
The Bedrock of Jacob: When Jacob's Faith Becomes His Own
GENESIS 28, 35

LESSON TWO: Your Forgiveness Comes from God's Steadfast Love
The Bedrock of Moses: When Moses Asks God's Forgiveness
EXODUS 34

LESSON THREE: Your Progress Comes from God's Power
The Bedrock of Joshua: When the Israelites Cross the Jordan River
JOSHUA 4

LESSON FOUR: Your Rescue Comes from Jesus' Resurrection
The Bedrock of Jesus: When the Stone Is Rolled Away from Jesus' Empty Tomb
MATTHEW 27–28

LESSON FIVE: Your Purpose Comes from the Church's Position
The Bedrock of the Church: When Peter Challenges Christians to Be like Christ
1 PETER 2

Learn more at thestorylineproject.com.

CP1836

Storyline Bible Studies

Each study follows people, places, or things throughout the Bible. This approach allows you to see the cohesive storyline of Scripture and appreciate the Bible as the literary masterpiece that it is.

Access free resources to help you teach or lead a small group at thestorylineproject.com.

Coming Soon: *Sinners* and *Saints*

NavPress

STORYLINE

Acknowledgments

WITHOUT MY FAMILY'S SUPPORT, the **Storyline Bible Studies** would just be a dream. I'm exceedingly grateful for a family that prays and cheers for me when I step out to try something new. To my husband, Aaron, son, Caleb, and mom, Noemi: You three sacrificed the most to ensure that I had enough time and space to write. Thank you. And to all my extended family: I know an army of Armstrongs was praying and my family in Austin was cheering me on to the finish line. Thank you.

To my ministry partners at the Polished Network, Integrus Leadership, and Dallas Bible Church: Linking arms with you made this project possible. I love doing Kingdom work with you.

NavPress and Tyndale teams: Thank you for believing in me. You wholeheartedly embraced the concept, and you've made this project better in every way possible. Special thanks to David Zimmerman, my amazing editor Caitlyn Carlson, Elizabeth Schroll, Olivia Eldredge, David Geeslin, and the entire editorial and marketing teams.

Jana Burson: You were the catalyst. Thank you.

Teresa Swanstrom Anderson: Thank you for connecting me with Caitlyn. You'll forever go down in history as the person who made my dreams come true.

All my friends rallied to pray for this project when I was stressed about the deadlines. Thank you. We did it! Without your intercession, these wouldn't be complete. I want to give special thanks to Lee, Sarah, Amy, Amy, Tiffany, and Jenn for holding up my arms to complete the studies.

Resources for Deeper Study

OLD TESTAMENT

Bearing God's Name: Why Sinai Still Matters by Carmen Joy Imes

The Epic of Eden: A Christian Entry into the Old Testament by Sandra L. Richter

NEW TESTAMENT

Echoes of Scripture in the Gospels by Richard B. Hays

The Gospels as Stories: A Narrative Approach to Matthew, Mark, Luke, and John by Jeannine K. Brown

BIBLE STUDY

Commentary on the New Testament Use of the Old Testament, eds. G. K. Beale and D. A. Carson

Dictionary of Biblical Imagery, eds. Leland Ryken, James C. Wilhoit, and Tremper Longman III

The Drama of Scripture: Finding Our Place in the Biblical Story by Craig G. Bartholomew and Michael W. Goheen

How (Not) to Read the Bible: Making Sense of the Anti-Women, Anti-Science, Pro-Violence, Pro-Slavery and Other Crazy Sounding Parts of Scripture by Dan Kimball

How to Read the Bible as Literature . . . and Get More Out of It by Leland Ryken

Literarily: How Understanding Bible Genres Transforms Bible Study by Kristie Anyabwile

The Mission of God: Unlocking the Bible's Grand Narrative by Christopher J. H. Wright

"Reading Scripture as a Coherent Story" by Richard Bauckham, in *The Art of Reading Scripture*, eds. Ellen F. Davis and Richard B. Hays

Reading While Black: African American Biblical Interpretation as an Exercise in Hope by Esau McCaulley

Read the Bible for a Change: Understanding and Responding to God's Word by Ray Lubeck

Scripture as Communication: Introducing Biblical Hermeneutics by Jeannine K. Brown

What Is the Bible and How Do We Understand It? by Dennis R. Edwards

Words of Delight: A Literary Introduction to the Bible by Leland Ryken

About the Author

KAT ARMSTRONG was born in Houston, Texas, where the humidity ruins her Mexi-German curls. She is a powerful voice in our generation as a sought-after Bible teacher. She holds a master's degree from Dallas Theological Seminary and is the author of *No More Holding Back*, *The In-Between Place*, and the **Storyline Bible Studies**. In 2008, Kat cofounded the Polished Network to embolden working women in their faith and work. Kat is pursuing a doctorate of ministry in New Testament context at Northern Seminary and is a board member of the Polished Network. She and her husband, Aaron, have been married for twenty years; live in Dallas, Texas, with their son, Caleb; and attend Dallas Bible Church, where Aaron serves as the lead pastor.

KATARMSTRONG.COM   **THESTORYLINEPROJECT.COM**
@KATARMSTRONG1   **@THESTORYLINEPROJECT**

Make peace with your past.
Find hope in the present.
Step into your future.

W Publishing Group
An Imprint of Thomas Nelson

Available everywhere books are sold.

Notes

INTRODUCTION

1. Matthew Sleeth, *Reforesting Faith: What Trees Teach Us about the Nature of God and His Love for Us* (Colorado Springs: Waterbrook, 2019), 17.
2. For example, see https://biblehub.com/hebrew/6086.htm.

LESSON ONE | CHOOSING WISELY INSTEAD OF TAKING MATTERS INTO YOUR OWN HANDS

1. "Bear Grylls," Penguin Books, accessed June 6, 2022, https://www.penguin.co.nz/authors/bear -grylls; and Bear Grylls (@beargrylls), "People sometimes ask me if my back ever hurts having broken it all those years ago . . .," Instagram photo, March 31, 2021, https://www.instagram.com/p /CNExdq5H7no.
2. Fleming Rutledge, *And God Spoke to Abraham: Preaching from the Old Testament* (Grand Rapids, MI: Eerdmans, 2011), 43.
3. John H. Sailhamer, *The Pentateuch as Narrative: A Biblical-Theological Commentary* (Grand Rapids, MI: Zondervan, 1992), 6.
4. Sailhamer, *Pentateuch as Narrative*, 4.
5. Walter Brueggemann, *Genesis: A Bible Commentary for Teaching and Preaching* (Louisville: Westminster John Knox Press, 1982), 45.
6. Terje Stordalen, *Echoes of Eden: Genesis 2–3 and Symbolism of the Eden Garden in Biblical Hebrew Literature* (Leuven, Belgium: Peeters, 2000), 468.
7. For more on living in harmony with God, see the "What's so eternal about life?" section in Marty Solomon, *Asking Better Questions of the Bible: A Guide for the Wounded, Wary, and Longing for More* (Colorado Springs: NavPress, 2023), 26–27.
8. Leland Ryken, James C. Wilhoit, and Tremper Longman III, eds., *Dictionary of Biblical Imagery: An Encyclopedic Exploration of the Images, Symbols, Motifs, Metaphors, Figures of Speech and Literary Patterns of the Bible* (Downers Grove, IL: InterVarsity Press, 1998), 889.

9. Jesudason Baskar Jeyaraj, "Genesis," in *South Asia Bible Commentary: A One-Volume Commentary on the Whole Bible*, ed. Brian Wintle (Grand Rapids, MI: Zondervan, 2015), 17.

10. Glenn Kreider, "Eve," in *Vindicating the Vixens: Revisiting Sexualized, Vilified, and Marginalized Women of the Bible*, ed. Sandra Glahn (Grand Rapids, MI: Kregel, 2017), 139.

11. BibleProject has a whole series of podcasts and videos devoted to the trees in the Bible. I've linked to them in the leader's guide for this Bible study. Scan the QR code on page xix to access it.

12. Sandra L. Richter, *The Epic of Eden: A Christian Entry into the Old Testament* (Downers Grove, IL: InterVarsity Press, 2008), 92–93.

13. Dru Johnson, *The Universal Story: Genesis 1–11*, Transformative Word series, eds. Craig G. Bartholomew and David Beldman (Bellingham, WA: Lexham Press, 2018), 49–50.

14. Sailhamer, *Pentateuch as Narrative*, 103.

15. Kreider, "Eve," in *Vindicating the Vixens*, 144.

LESSON TWO | TAKING NOTICE WHEN GOD IS TRYING TO GET YOUR ATTENTION

1. "Bonfire Memorial," Texas A&M University, accessed May 13, 2022, https://bonfire.tamu.edu.

2. Dennis T. Olson, "Exodus," in *Theological Bible Commentary*, eds. Gail R. O'Day and David L. Petersen (Louisville: Westminster John Knox Press, 2021), 29.

3. Tremper Longman III and Raymond B. Dillard, *An Introduction to the Old Testament*, 2nd ed. (Grand Rapids, MI: Zondervan, 2006), 74.

4. Matthew Sleeth, *Reforesting Faith: What Trees Teach Us about the Nature of God and His Love for Us* (Colorado Springs: Waterbrook, 2019), 71.

5. P. G. George and Paul Swarup, "Exodus," in *South Asia Bible Commentary: A One-Volume Commentary on the Whole Bible*, ed. Brian Wintle (Rajasthan, India: Open Door Publications, 2015), 82.

6. Richard Bauckham, *Who Is God? Key Moments of Biblical Revelation* (Grand Rapids, MI: Baker Academic, 2020), 37.

7. Nyasha Junior, "Exodus," in *Women's Bible Commentary*, 20th anniv. ed., eds. Carol A. Newsom, Sharon H. Ringe, and Jacqueline E. Lapsley (Louisville: Westminster John Knox Press, 2012), 59–60.

8. Ruth Haley Barton, *Strengthening the Soul of Your Leadership: Seeking God in the Crucible of Ministry* (Downers Grove, IL: InterVarsity Press, 2018), 37.

9. Carmen Joy Imes, *Bearing God's Name: Why Sinai Still Matters* (Downers Grove, IL: InterVarsity Press, 2019), 27.

10. Bauckham, *Who Is God?*, 42.

11. L. Michael Morales, *Exodus Old and New: A Biblical Theology of Redemption* (Downers Grove, IL: InterVarsity Press, 2020), 39.

12. Barton, *Strengthening the Soul of Your Leadership*, 63–64.

LESSON THREE | BRANCHING OUT FROM YOUR SHADY FAMILY TREE

1. Tim Mackie and Jon Collins, "Tree of Life (10 Episodes)," BibleProject podcast, accessed June 6, 2022, https://bibleproject.com/podcast/series/tree-life-podcast.

2. Matthew Sleeth, *Reforesting Faith: What Trees Teach Us about the Nature of God and His Love for Us* (Colorado Springs: Waterbrook, 2019), 128.

3. L. Juliana Claassens, "Isaiah," in *Theological Bible Commentary*, eds. Gail R. O'Day and David L. Petersen (Louisville: Westminster Knox Press, 2021), 211.

4. Tremper Longman III and Raymond B. Dillard, *An Introduction to the Old Testament*, 2nd ed. (Grand Rapids, MI: Zondervan, 2006), 313.

5. Fleming Rutledge, *And God Spoke to Abraham: Preaching from the Old Testament* (Grand Rapids, MI: Eerdmans, 2011), 302.

6. This saying isn't original to Jill Briscoe, but she famously spoke on this topic at the 2017 IF:Gathering. See "Episode 2: All the Way Home," Vimeo, accessed June 8, 2022, https://vimeo.com/406100459.

LESSON FOUR | STAYING CONNECTED TO JESUS FOR A FRUITFUL LIFE

1. Matthew Sleeth, *Reforesting Faith: What Trees Teach Us about the Nature of God and His Love for Us* (Colorado Springs: Waterbrook, 2019), 134.
2. Laura Clark, "Tree Grown from 2,000-Year-Old Seed Has Reproduced," *Smithsonian Magazine*, March 26, 2015, https://www.smithsonianmag.com/smart-news/tree-grown-2000-year-old-seed-has-reproduced-180954746.
3. John Roach, "'Methuselah' Palm Grown from 2,000-Year-Old Seed Is a Father," *National Geographic*, March 24, 2015, https://www.nationalgeographic.com/science/article/150324-ancient-methuselah-date-palm-sprout-science.
4. Beth Moore, *Chasing Vines: Finding Your Way to an Immensely Fruitful Life* (Carol Stream, IL: Tyndale, 2020), 142.
5. Moore, *Chasing Vines*, 134.
6. Richard B. Hays, *Echoes of Scripture in the Gospels* (Waco, TX: Baylor University Press, 2016), 336.
7. Tatiana, "The Great Exhaustion," Medium.com, December 29, 2021, https://medium.com/womentorship/the-great-exhaustion-c54cbf5750e4.
8. Blue Letter Bible, "Lexicon: Strong's G3306—*menō*," accessed June 7, 2022, https://www.blueletterbible.org/lexicon/g3306/niv/mgnt/0-1.
9. Moore, *Chasing Vines*, 127.
10. Moore, *Chasing Vines*, 127.
11. Hays, *Echoes of Scripture*, 337.
12. Marianne Meye Thompson, *John: A Commentary*, The New Testament Library (Louisville: Westminster John Knox Press, 2015), 325.

LESSON FIVE | REFRAMING YOUR PERSPECTIVE WITH VIEWS FROM THE TREETOPS

1. Gail R. O'Day, "Revelation," in *Theological Bible Commentary* (Louisville: Westminster John Knox Press, 2009), 471.
2. O'Day, "Revelation," in *Theological Bible Commentary*, 473.
3. Brian K. Blount, *Revelation: A Commentary*, The New Testament Library (Louisville: Westminster John Knox Press, 2009), 408.
4. Blount, *Revelation*, 408.
5. O'Day, "Revelation," in *Theological Bible Commentary*, 479.
6. Blount, *Revelation*, 374–75.
7. Leland Ryken, James C. Wilhoit, and Tremper Longman III, eds., *Dictionary of Biblical Imagery: An Encyclopedic Exploration of the Images, Symbols, Motifs, Metaphors, Figures of Speech and Literary Patterns of the Bible* (Downers Grove, IL: InterVarsity Press, 1998), 890.
8. Ryken, Wilhoit, and Longman, *Dictionary of Biblical Imagery*, 890.
9. Blount, *Revelation*, 375.